Richard L. Kellett

A Religious Masterpiece

The greatest devotional book ever written, the only book in the world to be translated as often and into as many languages as the Bible, this enduring and revered classic of the interior life presents the Christian dialogue between man and his Maker in a conversation that all may enjoy and from which everyone can profit. Thomas à Kempis, as witty a monk as he was holy and wise, lived six centuries ago, yet every word he wrote is as perceptively true today as it was then. He knows the hindrances and weaknesses man suffers in his lifelong effort to pursue the good life, and he shows the joy that intimacy with God can bring.

The genius of Thomas à Kempis lies principally in his simplicity, and anyone can find pleasure and enlightenment in *Of the Imitation of Christ*, whatever may be his faith or lack of it. This contemporary translation by Abbot Justin McCann is both readable and scholarly, and has been widely acclaimed by theologians as well as by the general public. It is likely to prove the definitive English text and should find an honored place in every home.

THIS IS A REPRINT OF THE HARDCOVER EDITION ORIGINALLY PUBLISHED BY BURNS OATES AND WASHBOURNE, LTD., PUBLISHERS TO THE HOLY SEE (LONDON) AND THE NEWMAN PRESS (WESTMINSTER, MARYLAND)

Of the
Imitation of Christ

In Four Books
by
Thomas à Kempis

Translated by
Abbot Justin McCann

A MENTOR RELIGIOUS CLASSIC
Published by **THE NEW AMERICAN LIBRARY**

Published as a MENTOR BOOK
By Arrangement with Burns Oates and Washbourne, Ltd.

FIRST PRINTING, MARCH, 1957
SECOND PRINTING, SEPTEMBER, 1959
THIRD PRINTING, AUGUST, 1960

First published in England in 1954 by Burns Oates and
Washbourne, Ltd., publishers to the Holy See,
and in the United States by the Newman Press.

MENTOR BOOKS are published by
The New American Library of World Literature, Inc.
501 Madison Avenue, New York 22, New York

PRINTED IN THE UNITED STATES OF AMERICA

SPECIAL INTRODUCTION TO THE
NEW AMERICAN LIBRARY (MENTOR) EDITION

For over five hundred years, the *Imitation* has been the most popular spiritual reading of the Christian world, and outside of the Bible is the most widely read religious book in the whole world. The *Imitation* was beloved by men as different as St. Thomas More and General Gordon; St. Ignatius Loyola and John Wesley; St. Francis Xavier and Dr. Samuel Johnson. Twenty years before its author, Thomas à Kempis, died at Zwolle in the Netherlands in 1471 aged over ninety, there were already extant more than 250 manuscript copies of his book; more than 700 are still in existence. The first printed edition appeared in Venice in 1472, a year after his death; by 1779 there were 1800 editions and translations; today no one has even attempted to count the current editions and there are translations into more than fifty languages. This new translation was first published in England in 1954 by Burns, Oates and Washbourne, Publishers to the Holy See, and in this country by The Newman Press of Westminster, Maryland.

So self-effacing was Thomas à Kempis that the earliest manuscripts are anonymous. In 1434 John de Bellerive, offering a copy of the book to the Brothers of the Common Life at Weisbach, said the author "did not wish to name himself." From 1447 on, Thomas is generally credited as author, although some twenty-five others have been suggested, including Saints Bernard and Bonaventure, Jean de Gerson, and Gerard Groote (or Groot), the founder of the Brothers of the Common Life. Jean de Gerson's name does appear on a 1460 manuscript, and on some later printed editions, but the style of the *Imitation* is generally conceded by scholars to match most closely that of Thomas's thirty-eight other works, even to the Dutch idioms. Thomas also wrote sermons, instructions to novices, and two biographies: a life of St. Lydwine, a Dutch saint famous for her illnesses, and a life of Gerard Groote. Only since 1924 has the latter been added to the suggested authors of the *Imitation,* because some scholars then put forward the theory that since the 1441 manuscript is an autograph in Thomas's own hand, it proves him to be but a copyist. (In the 1441 text, the book on the Eucharist becomes Book IV, although in earlier editions, and more logically, it was Book III.) Since none of the manuscripts of the *Imitation,* and none of the Brothers of the Common Life, ever ascribed its authorship to their founder, it seems unlikely that an ascription made five hundred years later could be correct. However, it *is* likely that some of Groote's own meditations, translated from Dutch into Latin, inspired chapters of Thomas's book and are enshrined in it.

It is hard to guess the why of bestsellers, but there can be no doubt that one of the reasons for the popularity of Thomas's own little book is its language. The Latin is rhythmical, almost poetic, and so simple that anyone who can read can understand it. Thomas, too, has been very lucky in his many translators. The present version, by Abbot Justin McCann, is both literal and literary, and its author, a well-known English scholar and an authority on spiritual literature, has worked from the 1441 definitive Latin text (the one in Thomas's own handwriting) in the Royal Library of Brussels. This translation is indeed likely to become the standard text of all English versions. Abbot McCann is titular Abbot of Westminster. Born in 1882, he went to school at Ampleforth, the great Benedictine school in the north of England, and after to Oxford, where he took first-class honors in classics in 1907. He was ordained priest in 1909. He has translated Karl Adam's *The Spirit of Catholicism* and Abbot Delattres's *Commentary on the Rule of St. Benedict* and has produced the classic English rendering of that rule itself. He has also edited *The Cloud of Unknowing* and the works of Father Augustine Baker.

The *Imitation*—which today would much better be called The *Following* of Christ because "imitate" has an apish connotation, whereas "follower" is an admirer seeking to assimilate the virtues of his leader—was written when modern Europe was emerging, at the time of the divorce between faith and reason, Church and State, layman and monk. Christendom had been a safe unit, the mainland, beyond which was only the sea or the vast desert. But Christendom gradually broke into separate islands, theologically, culturally, and morally ever more and more distinct and divided. The setting for the islands by the fourteenth century was no longer outer darkness or sterile sea, but an ever-increasing area neither holy nor sinful, but secular, a neutral "no man's land" which existed in every nation and state and empire: the realm of the layman.

The established institutions of the Church were inadequate to cope with the new situation, and sagged under the burden of infusing the new realm with Christian piety, and incorporating it into the mainland. Benedictine monasticism had become too propertied, the Franciscans were paralyzed by internal dissensions (could the disciples of the Poor Man of Assisi wear stockings, own books or shave?) and the great structure of medieval learning, that synthesis of lucid, logical thought and ordered prayer, was being frittered away by cavillings and carpings. William of Occam, for example, pared away faith from philosophy, and Meister Eckhart, the great German mystic, fled so far from reason into a personal experience of God that his words, if taken literally, would destroy the very meaning of faith itself.

Gerard Groote, in founding the Brothers of the Common Life, attempted to remedy these ills from within the Church, by joining ardent piety to classical learning, and by encouraging the reading of Scripture in small groups as part of the "modern devotion" associated with his name. The Brothers represent one of the first attempts to sanctify the whole of the new "lay" or "secular" or "neutral" area. They lived in the world, worked for their living, but met regularly together to foster their piety and to promote sound humanistic study. They set up schools, and among the men they trained were the great Cardinal, Nicolas of Cusa, Pope Hadrian VI, Erasmus the scholar and Copernicus the astronomer.

Thomas à Kempis was a priest whose order, the Canons Regular, was in close contact with the Brothers of the Common Life. Yet, since he was a monk, he was deeply suspicious of that "no man's land" in which the layman lives. His book seeks above all to hallow the whole man. It does not speak *of* God, but *to* God, about man. The sheer beauty of its unadorned truth is not a mirror to reflect, nor a painting to represent, the Light, but a clear window of flawless crystal. Through that window shines the Light of the words of the *Imitation* to illumine readers of all ages and all faiths.

——THE PUBLISHERS

PREFACE

Thomas à Kempis comes to us with a Latin name, which is to be translated "Thomas of Kempen." It was in that little Rhineland town, not far from Düsseldorf, that he was born, in the year 1379 or 1380, being the son of an artisan, by name John Haemerken. In his thirteenth year he was sent to school in the Netherlands, to the town of Deventer, whither his brother John, some fifteen years his senior, had preceded him. The busy cities of the Netherlands provided good teaching, and Deventer was besides a centre of Catholic piety, being the headquarters of a body of gifted and devout men, priests and layfolk, who were known as the Brothers of the Common Life. Their founder and moving spirit, Gerard Groot, was recently dead (1384); but his movement had survived him, finding a worthy leader in another priest of like gifts and devotion, by name Florentius Radewyn.

When Thomas reached Deventer, his brother John, who had joined the Canons Regular of Windesheim, entrusted him to the care of Florentius Radewyn. Master Florentius not only provided for the boy's lodging and education, but also by the example of his life exercised a strong influence upon him, drawing him into the devout circle over which he presided. Thus early in his career did Thomas come into intimate association with the devotional movement that was to determine the course and spirit of his life and to inspire his writings.

At the time when Thomas came to know the Brothers of the Common Life, their movement was in process of giving birth to a religious Congregation, of Canons Regular. A start had been made (1386) with a house at Windesheim, which lies some twenty miles north of Deventer and about four miles to the south-east of Zwolle. Such was the beginning of what became in the sequel the numerous and influential Congregation of Windesheim. Before Thomas finished his schooling, the Canons of Windesheim had embarked upon another foundation, at Mount St Agnes, near Zwolle. To supervise the new foundation, and to be its first prior, they sent John Haemerken (1398).

Consequently, when Thomas in his twentieth year, having completed his studies at Deventer, thought that he also was called to the religious life, it was natural that he should seek out his brother at Mount St Agnes and put his desire before him (1399). He was welcomed by John, but it would seem that it was some little time before the question of his vocation was decided, for we are told that it was not until the year 1408 that Thomas took his vows and became a full member of the Congregation. He was ordained priest in 1413.

From the first and throughout its course, Thomas's life at Mount St Agnes was a secluded one and in a secular sense quite uneventful. It was spent in the regular round of monastic duty, in much reading and study, in the copying or writing of books, and in the training of novices. Apart from his duties within the cloister, Thomas exercised his priesthood on behalf of the people who frequented the church, ministering to them at the altar, in the pulpit and in the confessional. No doubt he added in this way to his experience of men and women, and to his understanding of the troubles and trials of the soul. We are told of him that amidst his various occupations he was especially happy when he could retire for a while "to some nook with a book." When we consider the comprehensive and intimate knowledge of the Scriptures which his writings display, it is no wild conjecture to suppose that a favourite book on these occasions was the Bible itself.

It is part of the regular duty of a novice-master to give conferences to his novices, instructing them in every point of religious observance. Thomas was assiduous in the performance of this duty, and he took pains to give some of his conferences a permanent form, so that we can still read his *Sermons to Novices*. Besides this statutory work, Thomas found time to compose a variety of devout treatises, into which he put the spiritual teaching he had received from his own masters, the gleanings of his devout reading in the Scriptures and spiritual books, and the fruits of his personal experience. The *Imitation* is manifestly composed of these elements. Being a very modest person and regarding the pursuit of fame as no occupation for a devout Christian, Thomas set his name to none of his books and plainly cared not at all for his literary reputation. Without any thought of originality or personal merit, he sought only in writing the *Imitation* to compile out of the materials that lay to his hand an effective introduction to the devout life. But what he wrote, of whatever elements it be composed, is transfused by the ardour of his own devout spirit and possesses thereby an unmistakable power and charm. These things are to be regarded as eminently his own, and it is to them that is due in large measure the wide appeal of the *Imitation*.

When were the four treatises of the book first written? No precise answer can be given to this question. All that we can say is that there is evidence to support the belief that they were written and put into circulation round about the year 1425. Sixteen years later, i.e. in 1441, Thomas made a copy of these treatises (and of nine others), submitting the text to careful revision. This precious autograph has survived, being now among the manuscripts of the Royal Library of Brussels. Its text has been reproduced in facsimile (London, 1879) and has been several times printed. It is accepted as the definitive text of the *Imitation*, so that a translator of that book has no occasion to occupy himself with textual problems.

Although Thomas would appear to have issued the four treatises together, and although they are set side by side as the first four treatises of the autograph which has just been mentioned, yet he did not take the further step of providing a common title which should stamp these treatises as the four parts of a single work. However, as the book became more and more popular, such a common title was found for it in the first words of the first chapter-title, viz. *De Imitatione Christi* : Of the Imitation of Christ. An alternative title is suggested by the book's *incipit*, i.e. the first words of its text, *Qui sequitur me* : He that follows Me. We find these two things combined in the contemporary *Chronicle of Windesheim*, which was written by a fellow-canon and completed in the year 1464, seven years before the death of Thomas. The author of the *Chronicle*, John Busch, writing of the death of one of the canons, has this reference to Thomas and his book:

"It happened a few days before the death of the aforesaid canon that two well-known Brothers of our own Order from Mount St Agnes, near Zwolle, came to Windesheim to consult our Prior. One of these two was Brother Thomas à Kempis, a man of exemplary life, the author of *He that follows Me: of the imitation of Christ,* and of other devout books."

English practice may be said to have taken cognizance of both elements of this title, for some editors (the majority) have called the book *The Imitation of Christ,* whereas others have preferred *The Following of Christ.* The section-numbers within the chapters were provided in the seventeenth century by the learned Sommalius. His numbering is followed in this edition.

We left Thomas at Mount St Agnes, pursuing a quiet religious round and at the same time trying to compose his spiritual treatises. Returning now to the story of his life, we have very little more to record. For upwards of seventy years, with scarcely an interruption, Thomas lived thus at Mount St Agnes. He was in his ninety-second year when he died, on the first of May, 1471, after Compline.

CONTENTS

THE FIRST BOOK
COUNSELS FOR THE SPIRITUAL LIFE

THE SECOND BOOK
COUNSELS CALLING TO THE INNER LIFE

THE THIRD BOOK
OF INWARD CONSOLATION

Chapter	Page

THE FOURTH BOOK

A DEVOUT EXHORTATION TO HOLY COMMUNION

THE FIRST BOOK

COUNSELS
FOR THE SPIRITUAL LIFE

CHAPTER 1

OF THE IMITATION OF CHRIST AND CONTEMPT OF ALL THE VANITIES OF THE WORLD

H<small>E</small> *that follows Me shall not walk in darkness,* says the Lord. [1]

These are the words of Christ, by which we are urged to imitate His life and virtues, if we wish to be truly enlightened and freed from all blindness of heart.

Therefore, let it be our chief business to meditate upon the life of Jesus Christ.

2. The teaching of Christ excels all the teachings of the Saints; and if a man have His spirit, he shall find therein a hidden manna.

But it so happens that many hear the Gospel frequently and are little affected; because they lack the spirit of Christ. [2]

If you would understand Christ's words fully and taste them truly, you must strive to form your whole life after His pattern.

3. What good do you get by disputing learnedly about the Trinity, if you be lacking in humility and are therefore displeasing to the Trinity?

Verily, sublime words do not make a man holy and just; it is a virtuous life that makes him dear to God.

I would rather feel compunction than know how to define it.

If you knew the whole Bible by heart, and the sayings of all the philosophers, what would all that profit you without the love of God and His grace?

Vanity of vanities and all is vanity, [3] except loving God and serving Him only.

This is the highest wisdom: to despise the world and aim at the Kingdom of Heaven.

4. It is vanity therefore to seek perishable riches and to rely on them.

It is vanity also to pursue honours and raise yourself to a high dignity.

[1] John viii, 12.
[2] Romans viii, 9.
[3] Ecclesiastes i, 2.

It is vanity to follow the lusts of the flesh and to desire that which hereafter will bring grievous punishment.

It is vanity to wish for a long life and care little about a good life.

It is vanity to attend only to the present life, and not to look ahead to the future life.

It is vanity to love what quickly passes away, and not to be hastening thither where abides everlasting joy.

5. Often call to mind the proverb: *The eye is not sated with seeing, nor is the ear filled with hearing.*[1]

Study therefore to wean your heart from the love of visible things, and to attend rather to things invisible. For the man who indulges his sensual nature, sullies his conscience and loses the grace of God.

CHAPTER 2

OF HAVING A HUMBLE OPINION OF ONESELF

EVERY man naturally desires to know;[2] but what is the good of knowledge without the fear of God?

In fact, a poor peasant that serves God is better than a proud philosopher who neglects himself and ponders the courses of the stars.

He that knows himself well, becomes vile in his own eyes, and takes no delight in the praises of men.

If I knew everything in the world, yet had not charity,[3] what would it profit me in the sight of God, who will judge me according to my works?

2. Cease from the overweening desire of knowledge; because many distractions are found therein, and much delusion.

Learned men are very willing to seem wise, and to be called so.

Many are the items of knowledge which are of little or no good for the soul.

And he is very unwise who sets his mind on any other things than those which serve his salvation.

Many words do not satisfy the soul; but a good life gives ease to the mind, and a pure conscience affords great confidence before God.

3. The more you know and the better, so much the harder

[1] *Ibid.,* i, 8.
[2] Aristotle, *Metaphysics* i, 1.
[3] 1 Corinthians xiii, 2.

will your judgement be, unless your life also has been more holy.

∨ Be not then conceited for any skill or learning that you have; but rather be afraid for the knowledge that is given you.

If it seems to you that you know many things, and understand them well enough; yet recognise that there are many more things of which you are ignorant.

Be not high-minded,[1] but rather acknowledge your ignorance.

Why should you prefer yourself to another, when many may be found who are more learned than you and better skilled in the law?

∨If you desire a profitable sort of knowledge and learning, love to be unknown and to be esteemed as nothing.

4. This is the highest and most profitable lesson: truly to know and despise ourselves.

To think nothing of ourselves, and always to judge well and highly of others: this is great wisdom and perfection.

If you should see another openly do wrong, or commit some grievous sins, you ought not to think yourself better; for you know not how long you can persevere in well-doing.

We are all frail; but you shall deem none more frail than yourself.

CHAPTER 3

OF THE DOCTRINE OF TRUTH

HAPPY is the man whom truth teaches by itself, not by figures and passing words, but as it is in itself.

✓Our own way of thinking and our perception often deceive us, and they see but little.

What is the good of reasoning and disputing about dark and hidden things, when we shall not be censured at the Judgement for not knowing them?

Supreme folly! We neglect the things that are useful and necessary, and we willingly give our attention to those that are curious and mischievous. Having eyes we see not.[2]

2. And what have we to do with qualities and quiddities? If a man listens to the Eternal Word, he is delivered from a multitude of opinions.

From the one Word are all things, and all things speak of this One; and this is the Beginning, which also speaks to us.[3]

[1] Romans xi, 20.
[2] Psalm xciii, 5; Mark viii, 18.
[3] John viii, 25.

Without Him no man understands or judges rightly.

The man to whom all things are one, who refers all things to one, and sees all things in one: he can be steadfast in heart and abide peacefully in God.

O my God and my Truth! make me one with Thee in everlasting charity.

I am often wearied with reading and hearing many things; in Thee is all I wish or desire.

Let all teachers hold their peace, and all created things keep silence in Thy presence; do Thou alone speak to me.

3. The more a man is united within himself and inwardly simple, so much the more and deeper things does he understand without labour; for he receives the light of understanding from on high.

A man of pure, simple, and steadfast spirit is not distracted by the multitude of things he has to do; for he does all for the honour of God, and strives to keep himself inwardly free from all self-seeking.

Who does more hinder and trouble you than your own heart's unmortified affection?

A good and devout man first arranges inwardly the works he has to perform outwardly. Nor do those works draw him to indulge the desires of his lower nature; on the contrary, he constrains them to obey the dictates of right reason.

Who has a harder struggle than the man that strives to overcome himself?

But this ought to be our chief business, namely, to overcome self, and by daily gaining more mastery over self to grow better and better.

4. All perfection in this life is attended by some imperfection, and no speculation of ours is without a certain obscurity.

The humble knowledge of oneself is a surer way to God than profound learning.

Yet learning or any simple knowledge is not to be censured, because it is good in itself and ordained by God; but a good conscience and a virtuous life are always to be preferred.

But because many take more pains to know much than to live well, therefore they often go astray, and bear no fruit at all, or but little.

5. O if men would be as diligent in the rooting out of vices and engrafting of virtues as they are in mooting questions, there would not be so many evils and scandals among the people, nor such laxity in monasteries!

Truly, when the Day of Judgement comes, we shall not be

asked what we have read, but what we have done; not how well we have spoken, but how religiously we have lived.

Tell me, Where are all those doctors and masters with whom you were well acquainted while they were yet alive and famous for their learning?

Others now hold their preferments, and I know not that they ever think of them.

In their lifetime they seemed to be something, and now they are not spoken of.

6. O how quickly passes away the glory of the world! O that their life had been in keeping with their learning! Then would they have studied and lectured to good purpose.

How many perish in the world by vain learning, since they set small store upon the service of God.

And because they choose to be great rather than humble, therefore do they become vain in their speculations.[1]

He is truly great who has great love of God.

He is truly great who is little in his own eyes, and counts for nothing all the heights of honour.

He is truly prudent who esteems all earthly things as dung, that he may win Christ.[2]

And he is truly most learned, who does the will of God and forsakes his own.

CHAPTER 4

OF PRUDENCE IN WHAT WE DO

WE must not trust every word or impulse, but cautiously and patiently weigh the matter according to God.

Alas! we are so imperfect that we often believe and speak evil of our neighbours more readily than good.

But perfect men do not easily give credit to every tale-bearer; for they know that human frailty is prone to evil, and very apt to slip in speech.

2. It is great wisdom not to be headlong in our actions, and not to persist obstinately in our own opinions.

It is a part of this wisdom also not to believe everything men say, nor straightway to pour into the ears of others what we have heard or believed.

Take counsel of a wise and conscientious man, and seek rather to be instructed by one that is better, than to follow your own notions.

[1] Romans i, 21.
[2] Philippians iii, 8.

ood life makes a man wise according to God, and gives great experience.

The more humble any one is in heart, and the more submissive to God, so much the wiser will he be in all things, and the more at peace.

CHAPTER 5

OF READING THE HOLY SCRIPTURES

TRUTH is to be sought for in the holy Scriptures, not eloquence.

All holy Scripture should be read in the spirit in which it was written.

We should search the Scriptures for what is profitable to our souls and not for beauties of language.

We ought to read devout and simple books as willingly as those that are high and profound.

The authority of the writer should not affect you, whether he be of little or great learning; but let love of the plain truth lead you to read.

Ask not, Who said that? but consider what is said.

2. Men pass away, but the truth of the Lord abides for ever.[1]

God speaks to us in many ways, without respect of persons.

Our curiosity is often a hindrance to us in reading the Scriptures, when we wish to understand and to discuss what ought to be passed over in simplicity.

If you wish to derive profit, read with humility, with simplicity, and with faith; and seek not at any time the fame of being learned.

Do not hesitate to ask questions, and listen in silence to the words of holy men. Nor let the parables of the elders be displeasing to you, for they are not uttered without cause.

CHAPTER 6

OF INORDINATE AFFECTIONS

WHENEVER a man desires anything inordinately, at once he is disquieted within himself.

The proud and the covetous are never at rest; the poor and humble in spirit pass their life in abundance of peace.

[1] Psalm cxvi, 2.

If a man be not yet perfectly dead to self, he is soon tempted and overcome, and that even in petty and paltry matters.

He that is weak in spirit, and as yet somewhat carnal and inclined to things of sense, cannot without difficulty sever himself wholly from earthly desires.

And therefore he is often sad when he does withdraw himself; moreover, he is easily moved to anger if anyone thwarts him.

2. And, if he have achieved his desire, forthwith he is burdened with remorse of conscience for having gone after his passion; which does not help him at all to the peace he looked for.

It is by resisting the passions, and not by serving them, that true peace of heart is to be found.

There is no peace, therefore, in the heart of the carnal man, nor in the man who is devoted to outward things; but only in the fervent and spiritual man.

CHAPTER 7

OF AVOIDING VAIN HOPE AND PRIDE

HE is foolish that puts his hope in man, or in things created.

Be not ashamed to serve other men for the love of Jesus Christ, and to be looked upon as poor in this world.

Do not rely upon yourself, but put your trust in God.

Do what you are able to do, and God will assist your good will.

Put your trust neither in your own knowledge, nor in the cleverness of any man living, but rather in the grace of God, who helps the humble and humbles the presumptuous.

2. Glory not in riches, if you have them, nor in friends, because they are powerful, but in God who gives all things and above all desires to give you Himself.

Boast not of your stature, or of the beauty of your body, which a little sickness can spoil and disfigure.

Be not proud of your abilities or your talents, lest you offend God, to whom you owe whatever natural gifts you possess.

3. Do not think yourself better than others, lest perhaps you be accounted worse by God, who knows what is in man.[1]

Be not proud of your good works; for the judgements of God are other than the judgements of men, and often what pleases men displeases Him.

[1] John ii, 25.

If you have any good in you, believe still better things of others, that you may preserve humility.

It will do you no harm to put yourself below everybody; but it will hurt you very much to think yourself superior even to one other man.

The humble man dwells in continual peace; but the proud man's heart is the prey of envy and frequent anger.

CHAPTER 8

OF SHUNNING TOO GREAT FAMILIARITY

Do not open your heart to every man;[1] but discuss your affairs with one that is wise and fears God.

Be seldom with young people and strangers.

Do not fawn upon the rich, and be not fond of appearing in the presence of the great.

Keep company with the humble and simple, with the devout and well-ordered; and converse of such things as are edifying.

Be not familiar with any woman; commend all good women in general to God.

Desire to be familiar only with God and His holy Angels; and shun the acquaintance of men.

2. We should have charity towards all men; but familiarity is not expedient.

It sometimes happens that a person unknown to us has a good reputation and is much esteemed; and then we meet him, and the man himself proves far from pleasing.

Sometimes we think to please others with our company; whereas we begin rather to be displeasing to them, because of the evil that they discover in us.

CHAPTER 9

OF OBEDIENCE AND SUBJECTION

It is a very great thing to be in a state of obedience, to live under a superior and not to be one's own master.

It is much safer to live in subjection than in authority.

Many are under obedience rather out of necessity than out of love; and such as these suffer and are apt to murmur.

Neither will they acquire liberty of mind, unless they submit themselves with their whole heart for God's sake.

[1] Ecclesiasticus viii, 22.

Run here or there, you will find no rest but in humble subjection under the rule of a superior.

Many a man has conceived the notion that he would
be better somewhere else, and has been deluded by it.

2. Everyone likes to have his own way, and leans most to
those that agree with him.

But if God be amongst us, we must needs sometimes give
up our own opinion for the blessing of peace.

Who is so wise that he can fully know all things?

Be not over-confident therefore in your own opinions, but
be ready also with pleasure to hear those of others.

Although your opinion be right, yet if for God's sake you
abandon it and follow another man's you will profit the more.

3. For I have often heard that it is safer to hear and take
advice than to give it.

It may well happen also that each one's opinion is good.
But to be unwilling to acquiesce in the opinion of others,
when reason or occasion requires it, is a sign of pride and
obstinacy.

CHAPTER 10

OF AVOIDING UNNECESSARY TALKING

AVOID the concourse of men as much as you can; for the dis-
cussion of worldly affairs is very bad for the soul, even
though they be discussed with a good intention. For we are
quickly defiled and enslaved by vanity.

I wish I had often held my peace and had not been in the
company of men.

Why are we so fond of talking and of gossiping with one
another, though we seldom return to silence without some
wound to conscience?

The reason why we are so fond of talking is that we seek
consolation from one another by much chattering together, and
wish to ease our hearts that are wearied with distracting
thoughts.

And we are very fond of talking and thinking of those
things which we best love or desire, or those which we feel
to be against us.

2. But, alas! it is often vainly and to no purpose; for this
outward consolation greatly damages inward and divine consolation.

Therefore must we watch and pray,[1] lest time pass away fruitlessly.

If it be lawful and expedient to speak, speak of such things as will edify.

Evil habit and negligence about our spiritual advancement are largely responsible for our keeping no guard on our tongues.

Yet devout conferences upon spiritual things are no small help to spiritual progress, especially where persons of like mind and spirit are associated together in God.

CHAPTER 11

OF ACQUIRING PEACE AND ZEAL FOR SPIRITUAL PROGRESS

WE might have much peace, if we would not busy ourselves with the sayings and doings of other people, and with things that do not concern us.

How can he long remain at peace who mixes himself up with the concerns of others, who seeks distractions abroad, who is little or seldom inwardly recollected?

Blessed are the single-minded, for they shall enjoy much peace.

2. Why were some of the Saints so perfect and contemplative?

Because they strove to restrain themselves wholly from all earthly desires.

And so they were able to cleave to God with their innermost hearts, and to find time for attending to their souls.

But we are too much taken up with our own passions, and too solicitous about transitory things.

Seldom do we perfectly overcome one single vice; nor do we ardently desire to make daily progress; therefore we remain cold and lukewarm.

3. If we were perfectly dead to ourselves, and our hearts were not entangled, then might we relish divine things, and have some taste of heavenly contemplation.

The chief and greatest obstacle is that we are not free from passions and lusts, and strive not to enter upon the perfect way of the Saints.

When we meet with even a little adversity, we are immediately discouraged and turn to human consolation.

4. If we strove like valiant men to stand firm in the battle,

[1] Matthew xxvi, 41.

surely we should see God's help coming down to us from heaven.

For He is ready to help them that fight bravely and trust in His grace; and He Himself provides us occasions to fight, in order that we may conquer.

If we place our spiritual progress in outward observances only, our devotion will soon come to an end.

But let us lay the axe to the root,[1] so that, being purged of passions, we may possess our souls in peace.

5. If every year we rooted out one vice, we should soon become perfect men.

But now we often feel that things have gone the other way. We find that we were better and purer in the beginning of our religious life than we are after many years of profession.

Our fervour and progress ought to increase daily; but now it is thought a great thing if anyone can retain something of his first fervour.

If we would do ourselves a little violence in the beginning, then we should be able afterwards to do all things with ease and joy.

6. It is hard to give up old habits; it is harder still to resist our own will.

But if you do not overcome little and easy things, how will you surmount greater difficulties?

Resist your inclination in the beginning, and unlearn evil habit, lest by little and little it bring you into greater trouble.

O if you did but consider what peace you would procure for yourself, and what joy for others, by bearing yourself well, I think you would be more solicitous for your spiritual progress.

CHAPTER 12

OF THE USES OF ADVERSITY

IT is good for us at times to have troubles and adversities; for often they make a man enter into himself, so that he may know that he is in exile, and may not place his hopes in anything of this world.

It is good for us that we sometimes suffer contradictions, and that people think ill and poorly of us, even when we do and mean well.

Such things often help to humility and keep us from vainglory.

[1] Matthew iii, 10.

For then do we the more seek God for our inward witness, when outwardly we are slighted by men and incur discredit.

2. Therefore ought a man to establish himself so firmly in God that he has no need to seek many human consolations.

When a man of good will is afflicted or tempted or troubled with evil thoughts, then he understands better the great need he has of God; for he realizes that he can do no good without Him.

Then also he sighs and prays, by reason of the miseries he suffers.

Then is he weary of living longer, and wishes death to come, that he may be dissolved and be with Christ.[1]

Then also he well perceives that perfect security and full peace cannot be found in this world.

CHAPTER 13

OF RESISTING TEMPTATIONS

As long as we live in this world, we cannot be without trial and temptation.

Hence is it written in Job: *Man's life on earth is temptation.*[2]

Every one, therefore, should be solicitous about his temptations, and watch in prayer,[3] lest the devil find an opportunity to entrap him; for Satan never sleeps, but goes about, seeking whom he may devour.[4]

No one is so perfect and holy as not sometimes to have temptations; we can never be wholly free from them.

2. Nevertheless, temptations are often very profitable to us, troublesome and grievous though they be; for in them a man is humbled, purified, and instructed.

All the Saints passed through many tribulations[5] and temptations, and profited by them.

And they that could not endure temptations, became reprobate and fell away.

There is no order so holy nor place so retired that it is without temptations or adversities.

3. A man is never wholly secure from temptation as long as he lives; for since we were born with concupiscence, we have within us the source of temptation.

When one temptation or tribulation is over, another comes

[1] Philippians i, 23.
[2] Job vii, 1.
[3] 1 Peter iv, 7.
[4] 1 Peter v, 8.
[5] Acts xiv, 21.

on, and we shall always have something to suffer; for we have lost the blessing of our original felicity.

Many seek to fly temptations, and fall the more grievously into them.

By flight alone we cannot overcome; but by patience and true humility we become stronger than all our enemies.

4. He who only shuns them outwardly, and does not pluck out their roots, will profit little; nay, temptations will the sooner return, and he will find himself in a worse case than before.

Little by little, with long-suffering patience and God's help, you will overcome them better than by any force or violence of your own.

Take counsel the oftener in time of temptation, and do not for your part deal harshly with another when he is tempted. On the contrary, minister consolation, even as you would wish to be treated yourself.

5. All evil temptations take their beginning in fickleness of mind and lack of trust in God.

Just as a ship without a rudder is driven to and fro by the waves, so the careless and fickle man is variously tempted.

Fire tries iron and temptation a just man.

We often do not know what we can do; but temptation makes plain what we are.

We must be especially on our guard at the beginning of temptation. For the enemy is more easily overcome if at the start he be not suffered to pass the door of the mind. Let him be met outside, on the threshold, at the very moment he knocks.

Whence it has been said:

Resist beginnings; all too late the cure,
When ills have gathered strength by long delay.[1]

For first there comes into the mind a simple thought; then grows a vivid imagination; afterwards follow delectation, evil impulse, consent.

And so, by little and little, the malignant foe gains full entrance, when he is not resisted at the beginning.

And the longer any one has been slothful in resisting, so much the weaker he daily becomes in himself, and the enemy so much the stronger against him.

6. Some suffer heavier temptations in the beginning of their religious life, others in the end; and some there are who in a manner are troubled all their lifetime.

Some are quite lightly tempted, according to the wisdom and equity of the ordinance of God, who weighs man's condition and merits, and preordains all things for the salvation of His elect.

[1] Ovid, *Remedia Amoris* i, 91.

7. We must not, therefore, despair when we are tempted, but on that account pray the more fervently to God, that He would vouchsafe to help us in every tribulation. Of a truth, according to the saying of St. Paul, *He will make such issue with the temptation, that we may be able to bear it.*[1]

Let us, then, humble our souls under the hand of God[2] in every temptation and tribulation; for He will save and exalt the humble in spirit.

8. In temptations and tribulations is it proved what progress a man has made; and therein also there is greater merit, and virtue is made more manifest.

Nor is it a great thing if a man be devout and fervent when he feels no trouble; but if in time of adversity he suffers patiently, then will there be hope of much progress.

Some are preserved from great temptations and are often overcome in daily little ones. This is to humble them, so that they never presume upon themselves in great matters, who are found weak in things so small.

CHAPTER 14

OF AVOIDING RASH JUDGEMENT

TURN your eyes upon your own self, and see that you judge not the doings of others.

In judging others a man labours in vain, often goes astray, and easily sins; but in judging and scrutinizing himself, he always labours with profit.

We often judge of a thing according as we feel disposed towards it, and our judgement is distorted by our feelings.

If God were always the sole object of our desire, we should not be disturbed so easily when our views are not accepted.

2. It is often the case that there is some motive lurking within, or some influence concurring from without; and thus are we drawn along.

Many, in what they do, are really seeking themselves; yet they are not aware of that fact.

They seem also to be happy and at peace so long as things are done in accordance with their own will and judgement. But if anything happens otherwise than as they desire, then are they very quickly disturbed and saddened.

A difference in feelings and opinions too often gives rise

[1] 1 Corinthians x, 13.
[2] Peter v, 6.

to dissensions between friends and neighbours, and between religious and devout persons.

3. An old habit is with difficulty abandoned; and no man is willingly led further than he himself can see.

If you rely more on your own reason or industry than on the subduing power of Jesus Christ, seldom and late will you become an enlightened man.

For God wills us to be perfectly subject to Himself, and to transcend all reasoning by the ardour of our love.

CHAPTER 15

OF WORKS DONE OUT OF CHARITY

EVIL ought not to be done for anything in the world, nor for the love of any human being; but yet, for the benefit of one that is in need, a good work is sometimes freely to be left undone, or rather to be changed for a better. For by this means a good work is not lost, but changed into a better.

Without charity, the outward work profits nothing; but whatever is done out of charity, be it never so little and contemptible, becomes wholly fruitful. For God weighs the love with which a man works rather than how much work he does.

2. He does much who loves much; he does much who does well what he does; he does well who serves the common good rather than his own will.

Often that seems to be charity which is rather carnality; for natural inclination, self-will, hope of reward, study of our own interest — these things will seldom be absent.

3. He that has true and perfect charity seeks himself in nothing, but desires only that God be glorified in all things.

And he envies no man; for he is in love with no private joy of his own, nor desires to rejoice in himself. But his desire is to find his happiness in God, above every other good thing.

He attributes no good to any creature, but refers it all to God, from whom as from their fountain all things proceed; and in whom finally all the Saints do rest, in the joy of fruition.

O if a man had but a spark of real charity, he would surely perceive that all earthly things are full of vanity!

CHAPTER 16

OF BEARING THE DEFECTS OF OTHERS

WHATEVER a man cannot amend in himself or in others, he ought to bear with patience, until God ordains otherwise.

Consider that perhaps it is better so, for your probation and to exercise you in patience, without which our merits are not greatly to be esteemed.

Nevertheless, when you have such hindrances, you should pray that God would deign to help you, and that you may be able to bear them cheerfully.

2. If any one, being once or twice admonished, does not comply, do not contend with him, but leave it all to God, that His will may be done, and He be honoured in all His servants; for He knows how to turn evil into good.

Study to be patient in bearing the defects and infirmities of others, of what kind soever; for you also have many things which others must endure.

If you cannot make yourself such as you would be, how can you expect to have another exactly to your mind?

We would fain see others perfect, and yet we do not amend our own faults.

3. We would have others strictly corrected, and we are unwilling to be corrected ourselves.

The large liberty of others displeases us, and yet we ourselves will not be denied anything we ask.

We wish others to be restricted by rules, and we ourselves can no longer bear to be checked in the least.

And so it is clear how seldom we weigh our neighbour in the same balance as ourselves.

If we were perfect, what then should we have to bear with from others for the love of God?

4. But now God hath thus ordered it, that we may learn to bear one another's burdens.[1] For no one is without defect, no one without his burden; no one is sufficient for himself, no one is wise enough for himself; but we must bear with one another, comfort one another, help, instruct, and admonish one another.

But the measure of each man's virtue is best seen in occasions of adversity.

For adversities do not make a man frail; they show what sort of man he is.

[1] Galatians vi, 2.

CHAPTER 17

OF THE MONASTIC LIFE

You must learn to overcome yourself in many things, if you would have peace and concord with others.

It is no small thing to dwell with brethren in a monastery, and to live there without complaint, and to persevere faithfully even to death.

Blessed is he who shall have lived there well, and have made a happy end.

If you would persevere dutifully and make progress, look on yourself as an exile and a pilgrim upon earth.[1]

You must become a fool for Christ's sake,[2] if you wish to lead the life of a religious.

2. The habit and the tonsure effect but little; but the moral change, and the entire mortification of the passions: these make a true religious.

He that seeks anything else but simply God and the salvation of his soul, will find nothing but trouble and sorrow.

And he who does not strive to be the least, and subject to all, cannot long remain in peace.

3. You have come to serve, not to govern. Know that your vocation is to suffer and to labour, not to pass your time in idleness or vain conversation.

Here, therefore, men are tried as gold in the furnace.

Here no man can abide, except he be ready with all his heart to humble himself for the love of God.

CHAPTER 18

OF THE EXAMPLES OF THE HOLY FATHERS

Look upon the lively examples of the holy Fathers, in whom shone real perfection and religion, and you will see how little it is that we are doing, yes, almost nothing.

Alas, what is our life, if it be compared with theirs?

Saints and friends of Christ, they served our Lord in hunger and thirst, in cold and nakedness, in labour and weariness, in watchings and fastings, in prayers and holy meditations, in frequent persecutions and reproaches.[3]

[1] 1 Peter ii, 11.
[2] 1 Corinthians iv, 10.
[3] 2 Corinthians xi, 26, 27.

2. O how many and grievous tribulations did the Apostles suffer, and the Martyrs, and Confessors, and Virgins, and all the rest who resolved to follow the steps of Christ!

For they hated their lives in this world, that they might keep them to life eternal.[1]

O what a strict and self-renouncing life the holy Fathers of the desert led! what long and grievous temptations they bore! how often were they harassed by the enemy! what frequent and fervent prayers they offered to God! what rigorous abstinence they practised! how great was their zeal and fervour for spiritual progress! what a valiant contest they fought to overcome their faults! how pure and upright an intention they kept towards God!

By day they laboured, and in the night they gave themselves to long prayers; although, even while they laboured, they ceased not from mental prayer.

3. They spent all their time profitably; every hour seemed short which they spent with God; and even their necessary bodily nourishment was forgotten in the great sweetness of contemplation.

They renounced all riches, dignities, honours, friends, and kindred; they desired to have nothing of this world; they hardly took what was necessary for life; it grieved them to serve the body even in its necessities.

Accordingly, they were poor in earthly things, but very rich in grace and virtues.

Outwardly they suffered want, but within they were refreshed with grace and divine consolation.

4. They were aliens to the world; but they were the very near and familiar friends of God.

To themselves they seemed as nothing, and the world despised them; but they were precious and beloved in the eyes of God.

They persevered in true humility, they lived in simple obedience, they walked in charity and patience; and so every day they advanced in spirit, and gained great favour with God.

They were given for an example to all religious; and they ought more to excite us to advance in good, than should the number of the lukewarm make us grow lax.

5. O how great was the fervour of all religious in the beginning of their holy institute!

How great was their devotion in prayer! how great their zeal for virtue! how strong the discipline that was observed! what reverence and obedience, under the rule of the superior, flourished in all!

[1] John xii, 25.

Their traces that remain still bear witness that they were truly holy and perfect men, who did battle so stoutly and trampled the world under their feet.

Now he is thought great who is not a transgressor and can endure with patience the life he has undertaken.

6. O the lukewarmness and negligence of our state! that we so soon fall away from our first fervour, and even grow weary of life, because of our slothfulness and tepidity.

Would to God that the desire to grow in virtue may not go quite asleep in you, who have so often seen the many examples of the devout!

CHAPTER 19

OF THE EXERCISES OF A GOOD RELIGIOUS

THE life of a good religious ought to abound in every virtue, that he may be such inwardly as he seems to men outwardly.

And indeed he ought to be much more within than he appears outwardly; for God is our Beholder, and we should exceedingly stand in awe of Him, wherever we may be, and like the Angels walk before Him in purity.

Every day we ought to renew our purpose and rouse ourselves to fervour, as if that day were the first day of our conversion.

And we ought to say, Help me, O Lord God, in my good purpose, and in Thy holy service, and grant that I may this day begin indeed, since what I have hitherto done is nothing.

2. As our purpose is, so will our progress be; and he has need of much diligence that wishes to advance much.

And if he who strongly purposes nevertheless often fails, what will he do that seldom or but weakly resolves?

Yet the falling off from any good resolution happens many ways; and a trifling omission in our exercises hardly passes over without some loss.

The resolutions of the just depend rather on the grace of God than on their own wisdom; and in Him they always put their trust, whatever they take in hand.

For man proposes, but God disposes; neither is the way of man in his own hands.

3. If, for piety's sake or a brother's benefit, an accustomed exercise be sometimes omitted, it can easily be resumed afterwards.

But if it be laid aside lightly, out of weariness of mind or negligence, it is no small fault and will be found to do harm.

Let us try as much as we can, we shall still readily fail in many things.

Nevertheless, we should always have some certain resolution, and especially against the things that are our greatest hindrances.

We must examine and set in order both our inner life and our outward behaviour, for both are of importance for our advancement in virtue.

4. If you cannot be continually recollected, at all events be so sometimes, and at least once a day: in the morning, for example, or in the evening.

In the morning make your resolution; in the evening examine your conduct, how you have behaved this day in word, deed, and thought; for it may be that in these you have many times offended God and your neighbour.

Gird yourself up like a man to resist the wicked suggestions of the devil; bridle gluttony, and you will the easier bridle every inclination of the flesh.

Never be wholly idle, but either reading, or writing, or praying, or meditating, or labouring at something for the common good.

Nevertheless bodily exercises are to be practised with discretion, and not equally to be undertaken by all.

5. Those things which are not common to all ought not to be done in public; for private devotions are more safely practised in secret.

You must take care not to shirk what is common and be too ready to do what is singular; but when you have fully and faithfully fulfilled all duties and orders, then, if there be any time left, give yourself to yourself, as your devotion may lead you.

All cannot use the self-same exercise; for one suits this person better, another that.

Moreover, according to the diversity of times are different exercises agreeable: some please on feast days, others suit better on common days.

We have need of one sort in time of temptation, of another in time of peace and quiet.

There are some things we love to think of when we are sad, and others when we are joyful in the Lord.

6. About the time of the principal festivals we should renew our good exercises, and implore more fervently the intercession of the Saints.

From festival to festival we should make our resolutions, as if we were then to depart from this world and to come to the eternal festival.

And so we ought to prepare ourselves carefully in seasons of devotion, and walk more devoutly, and keep every observance more strictly, as though we were soon to receive from God the reward of our labour.

7. And if it be put off, let us believe that we are not well enough prepared, and are as yet unworthy of that great glory which shall be revealed in us[1] at the time appointed; and let us study to prepare ourselves better for our departure.

We read in St. Luke's Gospel: *Blessed is that servant, whom his lord when he comes shall find watching. Amen I say unto you, he shall set him over all his goods.*[2]

CHAPTER 20

OF THE LOVE OF SOLITUDE AND SILENCE

SEEK a convenient time to retire into yourself; and think often on the benefits of God.

Let curiosities alone; and read such books as turn the heart to compunction, rather than entertain the mind.

If you will refrain from superfluous talk and idle visits, and from giving ear to news and gossip, you will find yourself with sufficient and suitable time for good meditations.

The greatest Saints shunned the company of men when they could, and chose rather to live to God in secret.

2. There was one who said : *As often as I have been amongst men, I have returned home less a man.*[3] This we too often experience when we talk long.

It is easier to keep silence altogether than not to speak too much.

It is easier to keep retired at home than to be enough upon one's guard abroad.

He, therefore, who aims at inward and spiritual things, must with Jesus turn aside from the crowd.[4]

No man can safely appear in public but he who loves seclusion.

No man can safely speak but he who loves silence.

No man can safely be a superior but he who loves to live in subjection.

[1] Romans viii, 18.
[2] Luke xii, 43.
[3] Seneca, *Epistle* vii.
[4] John v, 13; Luke v, 16.

No man can safely command but he who has learned how to obey well.

3. No man can rejoice securely but he who has within him the testimony of a good conscience.

Yet the security of the Saints was always full of the fear of God.

Neither were they the less careful and humble in themselves because they shone with great virtue and grace.

But the security of the wicked arises from their pride and presumption, and in the end turns to their own deception.

Never promise yourself security in this life, however good a religious or devout solitary you may seem to be.

4. Often those highest in men's estimation have been in the greater danger, by reason of their excessive self-confidence.

Therefore it is better for many not to be wholly free from temptations, but to be often assaulted, lest they become too secure, lest they be puffed up with pride, lest they even turn aside too freely after outward consolations.

O how good a conscience would he keep, who never sought transitory joys, and never busied himself with the world!

O how great peace and tranquillity would he have, who should cut off all vain solicitude, and think only of the things of God and his salvation, and place his whole hope in God!

5. No one is worthy of heavenly consolation who has not diligently exercised himself in holy compunction.

If you would feel compunction to your very heart, retire to your room and shut out the noise of the world; as it is written, *Be ye contrite in your rooms.*[1]

You will find in your cell what you will too often lose abroad.

A cell constantly occupied grows sweet; whereas, if you frequent it little, it produces weariness.

If, from the beginning of your religious life, you occupy it and keep it well, it will be to you afterwards as a dear friend and most delightful solace.

6. In silence and in quiet the devout soul makes progress, and learns the hidden things of Scripture.

There she finds floods of tears, wherein each night she may wash and be cleansed. She shall become the more familiar with her Creator, the further she dwells from all the tumult of the world.

For whoso withdraws himself from his acquaintances and friends, to him will God draw near with His holy Angels.

It is better to lie hid and take diligent care of yourself, than neglecting yourself to work signs and wonders.

[1] Psalm iv, 5.

It is praiseworthy for a religious to go abroad but seldom, to shun being seen, and not even to desire to see men.

7. Why do you wish to see what it is not lawful for you to have? *The world passes away and the concupiscence thereof.*[1]

The desires of the senses draw you to roam abroad; but when the hour has passed away, what do you bring back with you but a weight upon your conscience and a dissipated heart?

A cheerful outing often begets a sorrowful home-coming; and a merry evening makes a sad morning.

So all carnal joys enter pleasantly; but in the end they bring remorse and destruction.

What can you see elsewhere that you do not see here? Lo, here are the heavens and the earth and all the elements; and out of these all things are made.

8. What can you see anywhere that can last long under the sun?

You think that your heart will be satisfied; but you will never be able to attain satisfaction.

If you could see all things at once before you, what would it be but an empty vision?

Lift up your eyes to God on high, and ask pardon for your sins and negligences.

Leave vain things to vain people; look rather to those things which God has commanded you.

Shut your door upon you,[2] and call to you Jesus your beloved.

Stay with Him in your cell; for nowhere else shall you find so great peace.

Had you never left your cell, to lend your ear to idle talk, you would have remained the better in true peace.

But because it is sometimes your pleasure to listen to news, you must needs suffer disquietude of heart.

CHAPTER 21

OF COMPUNCTION OF HEART

If you wish to make progress, keep yourself in the fear of God. Be not too free, but restrain all your senses under discipline, and do not abandon yourself to foolish mirth.

Give yourself to compunction of heart and you shall find devotion.

[1] 1 John ii, 17.
[2] Matthew vi, 6.

Compunction discloses much good, which dissipation quickly destroys.

It is wonderful that any man can ever abandon himself wholly to joy in this life, when he considers and ponders his state of exile and the manifold perils of his soul.

2. Through levity of heart and neglect of our defects we do not perceive the ills of our soul, but often vainly laugh when in all reason we should weep.

There is no true liberty or sound joy but in the fear of God with a good conscience.

Happy is the man that can put aside all the hindrance of distraction, and recollect himself in the unity of holy compunction.

Happy the man who renounces whatever may stain or burden his conscience.

Strive manfully; habit is overcome by habit.

If you can let men alone, they will let you alone, to do whatever you have to do.

3. Busy not yourself with other men's concerns; nor meddle with the business of your superiors.

Always keep an eye upon yourself first of all, and admonish yourself rather than any of your dearest friends.

If you have not the favour of men, be not thereby afflicted; but let it seriously concern you that you do not carry yourself so well and circumspectly as becomes a servant of God and a devout religious.

It is often better and safer for a man not to have many consolations in this life, especially such as are according to the flesh. Still, that we have not divine consolation, or experience it seldom, is our own fault; because we do not seek compunction of heart, and do not wholly renounce vain and outward consolations.

4. Recognize that you are unworthy of heavenly consolation and rather deserve much tribulation.

When a man has perfect compunction, then the whole world is burdensome and distasteful to him.

A good man finds abundant matter for sorrow and tears.

For whether he considers himself, or thinks of his neighbour, he knows that no man lives here below without tribulation.

And the more strictly he considers himself, the greater is his sorrow.

The subjects of just sorrow and interior compunction are our sins and vices, in which we lie so enwrapped that we are seldom able to contemplate heavenly things.

5. Did you think oftener of your death than of a long life, assuredly you would be more zealous to amend yourself.

Did you also ponder well the future pains of hell or purgatory, I think you would willingly bear labour and sorrow,
and fear no kind of austerity.

But because these things do not reach the heart, and we
still love the things that flatter us, therefore we remain cold
and very sluggish.

6. Often it is mere cowardice that makes the wretched body
complain so lightly.

Pray therefore humbly to the Lord to give you the spirit of
compunction. And say with the Prophet: *Feed me, O Lord,
with the bread of tears, and give me abundance of tears to
drink.*[1]

CHAPTER 22

OF THE CONSIDERATION OF HUMAN MISERY

WRETCHED are you, wheresoever you be and whithersoever
you turn, unless you turn to God.

Why are you troubled because things do not go with you as
you wish and desire? Who is there that has all things according to his will? Neither I, nor you, nor any man upon earth.

There is no man in the world without some trouble or trial,
be he King or Pope.

Who, then, is the best off? Assuredly he that is able to suffer
something for God's sake.

2. Weakminded and silly people often say: See what a
happy life that man leads! how rich he is, how great, how
powerful and exalted!

But take heed to heavenly riches, and you will see that all
these temporal ones are nothing; yes, most uncertain, and
rather burdensome than otherwise, since they are never possessed without anxiety and fear.

Man's happiness does not consist in having temporal things
in abundance; a moderate portion is sufficient for him.

Truly it is a misery to live upon the earth.

The more a man desires to be spiritual, the more distasteful
does this present life become to him; for he the better understands and more clearly sees the defects of human corruption.

For to eat, to drink, to watch, to sleep, to rest, to labour,
and to be subject to the other necessities of nature: this truly
is a great misery and affliction to a devout man, who would
gladly be set loose and free from all sin.

[1] Psalm lxxix, 6.

3. For the spiritual man is greatly weighed down in this world by the necessities of the body.

Hence the Prophet devoutly prays that he may be free from them, saying: *From my necessities deliver me, O Lord.*[1]

But woe to them that know not their own misery; and still more woe to them that make this wretched and perishable life the object of their love!

For some there are who cling to it so closely (though even by labouring or by begging they hardly have bare necessaries) that could they live here always, they would care nothing for the Kingdom of God.

4. O senseless men and unbelieving in heart, who lie so deeply sunk in earthly things that they relish nothing but what is carnal!

Miserable men! Yet a little while and they will realize to their cost that the thing they loved was a worthless thing and the merest nothing.

But the Saints of God, and all devoted friends of Christ, looked not to what pleases the flesh, nor to what flourishes for the time of this mortal life; but in all their hopes and aims they yearned after the good things that are eternal.

All their desire tended upwards, to the abiding and invisible things, lest by the love of things visible they should be dragged down to the lowest depths.

Lose not, brother, your confidence of making spiritual progress; you still have time, the hour is not yet passed.

5. Why will you put off your purpose from day to day? Arise, and begin this very instant! Say to yourself: Now is the time to be doing; now is the time to be fighting; now is the fit time to be amending my life.

When you are ill at ease and in tribulation, then is the time to win merit.

You must pass through fire and water before you come to the place of refreshment.

Except you do violence to yourself, you shall not overcome vice.

So long as we carry this frail body, we cannot be free from sin, nor live without weariness and sorrow.

Fain would we be at rest from all misery; but since by sin we have lost our innocence, we have lost also true happiness.

We must therefore have patience, and await God's mercy, till this iniquity pass away,[2] and mortality be swallowed up by life.[3]

[1] Psalm xxiv, 17.
[2] Psalm lvi, 2.
[3] Corinthians v, 4.

6. O how great is human frailty, which is ever prone to vice!

To-day you confess your sins, and to-morrow you again commit the sins you confessed.

Now you resolve to be on your guard, and an hour after you are acting as if you had made no resolution.

Justly then may we humble ourselves, and never think anything great of ourselves; since we are so frail and unstable.

And very soon may we lose by our negligence what we have scarce managed to gain by grace, and that at long last and after much labour.

7. What will become of us in the end, if we begin so early to grow lukewarm?

Woe to us if we turn aside to rest, as though already there were peace and security, when as yet our behaviour shows no trace of true holiness!

We ought, indeed, to become novices once again and be instructed in good behaviour; for then there might be some hope of future amendment and of greater spiritual progress.

CHAPTER 23

OF MEDITATION UPON DEATH

A very little while and all will be over with you here. Ask yourself are you ready for the next life. Man is to-day, and to-morrow he is gone.

And when he is out of sight, he is quickly also out of mind.

O the dullness and the hardness of the human heart, that dwells only upon things present, instead of providing rather for those which are to come!

You should so order yourself in every deed and thought as though you were to die this day.

If you had a good conscience, you would not much fear death.

It were better to avoid sin than to fly death.

If you are not prepared to-day, how will you be to-morrow?

To-morrow is an uncertain day; and how do you know if you shall have to-morrow?

2. Of what use is it to live long, when we amend ourselves so little?

Long life does not always amend us; on the contrary, it often increases our guilt.

Would that we had well spent even one day in this world!

Many count the years of their religious life; but often there is little fruit of amendment.

If it is a fearful thing to die, it will perhaps be more dangerous to live longer.

Blessed is the man that has the hour of his death continually before his eyes, and every day gets ready to die.

If you have ever seen a man die, reflect that you too will travel the same road.

3. When it is morning, think that you will not live till evening.

And when evening comes, venture not to promise yourself the next morning.

Therefore be always ready; and so live that death may never find you unprepared.

Many die suddenly and when they look not for it; for, *at an hour when we think not, the Son of man will come.*[1]

When that last hour shall come, then will you begin to have a far different opinion of all your past life; and great will be your grief that you have been so negligent and remiss.

4. How happy and how prudent is he who strives to be in life what he would fain be found in death!

For a perfect contempt of the world, a fervent desire to advance in virtue, the love of discipline, the labour of penance, readiness of obedience, self-denial, and the bearing of any kind of adversity for the love of Christ: these things will give us great confidence of dying happily.

Many are the good works you can do whilst in health; but when you are sick, I know not what you will be able to do.

Few are improved by sickness; so also they that go much on pilgrimage seldom grow in sanctity.

5. Do not trust in your friends and neighbours and leave your soul's welfare till hereafter; for men will forget you sooner than you think.

It is better to make provision in your lifetime and to send some good before you, than to trust to the assistance of others after death.

If you are not solicitous for yourself now, who will be solicitous for you hereafter?

Now is time very precious. *Lo, now is the acceptable time; lo, now is the day of salvation.*[2]

But, alas that you do not make better use of this time, when you might be meriting life eternal!

The time will come when you will desire one day or even one hour for amendment; and I know not if you will obtain it.

6. Ah, beloved! from how great danger can you free yourself, from how great fear deliver yourself, if only you be always fearful, and mindful of death.

[1] Matthew xxiv, 44; Luke xii, 40.
[2] 2 Corinthians vi, 2.

Therefore, study so to live now that in the hour of death you may be able to rejoice rather than be afraid.

Learn now to die to the world, that then you may begin to live with Christ.[1]

Learn now to despise all things, that then you may go freely to Christ.

Chastise your body now by penance, that then you may have sure confidence.

7. Ah, fool! why do you count on living long, when you are not sure of a single day?

How many thinking to live long have been deceived, and snatched unexpectedly from life!

How often have you heard it related that such a one fell by the sword, another was drowned, another falling from a height broke his neck, this man died at table, that other came to his end at play.

One perished by fire, another by the sword, another by pestilence, another at the hands of robbers. And thus death is the end of all, and man's life suddenly passes away, like a shadow.[2]

8. Who will remember you when you are dead? and who will pray for you?

Do now, beloved, do now all that you can; for you know not when you are to die, neither do you know what will befall you after death.

Whilst you have time, amass for yourself everlasting riches.[3]

Think of nothing but your salvation; care only for the things of God.

Make to yourself friends now, by venerating the Saints of God and imitating their lives, so that when you fail in this life they may receive you into everlasting dwellings.[4]

9. Keep yourself as a pilgrim and a stranger[5] upon earth, as one who has no concern with the business of the world.

Keep your heart free and lifted up to God, for here you have no lasting city.[6]

Send thither your prayers and daily sighs, with tears, that after death your spirit may merit to pass happily to the Lord. Amen.

[1] Romans vi, 8.
[2] Job xiv, 2.
[3] Matthew vi, 20; Luke xii, 33.
[4] Luke xvi, 9.
[5] 1 Peter ii, 11.
[6] Hebrews xiii, 14.

CHAPTER 24

OF JUDGEMENT
AND THE PUNISHMENTS OF SINNERS

IN all things look to the end, and consider that you shall stand before the strict Judge, from whom there is nothing hid; who takes no bribes, and receives no excuses, but will judge that which is just.

O wretched and foolish sinner, who are sometimes afraid of the countenance of an angry man! what answer will you make to God who knows all your evil deeds?

Why do you not make provision for yourself against the Day of Judgement, when no man can be excused or defended by another, but each one will have enough to do to answer for himself?

Now is your labour profitable, your tears acceptable, your groans heard, your sorrow satisfactory before God and availing to cleanse your soul.

2. The patient man has a great and wholesome purgatory; who, suffering wrongs, is more sorrowful for another's malice than for the injury to himself; who prays gladly for his adversaries, forgiving their offenses from his heart; who delays not to ask pardon of others; who is sooner moved to pity than to anger; who does frequent violence to himself, and strives to bring his flesh wholly into subjection to the spirit.

It is better to purge away our sins and cut off our vices now, than to keep them for purgation hereafter.

Truly we deceive ourselves, through the inordinate love we bear the flesh.

3. What else will that fire feed upon but your sins?

The more you spare yourself now and follow the flesh, so much the more dearly shall you pay for it hereafter; and the more fuel do you lay up for that fire.

In what things a man has sinned, in those things shall he be the more grievously punished.

There the slothful shall be pricked with burning goads, the gluttonous tormented with extreme hunger and thirst. There the lustful and the lovers of pleasure shall have burning pitch and stinking brimstone rained upon them; and the envious, like mad dogs, shall howl with pain.

4. There is no vice but shall have its own peculiar torment. There the proud shall be filled with all confusion, and the avaricious pinched with the most miserable penury.

There one hour of punishment shall be more grievous than a hundred years of the most bitter penance here.

There is no rest there, nor comfort, for the damned;[1] whereas here we have some respite from labour, and enjoy the comfort of our friends.

Be solicitous and sorry for your sins now, that in the Day of Judgement you may be safe with the blessed. *For then the just shall stand with great constancy against those that have afflicted and oppressed them.*[2]

Then shall he stand up to judge who now humbly submits himself to the judgements of men.

Then shall the poor and humble have great confidence, but the proud shall be encompassed with fear.

5. Then will it appear that he was wise in this world, who for Christ's sake learned to be a fool and despised.[3]

Then every tribulation borne with patience shall be pleasing, and all iniquity shall stop her mouth.[4]

Then shall every devout man rejoice, and all the ungodly shall mourn.

Then shall the flesh exult that was afflicted, more than if it had always been fed on dainties.

Then shall the mean habit shine, and the fine garment be tarnished.

Then shall the poor cottage be praised above the gilded palace.

Then shall enduring patience more avail than all the power of the world.

Then shall simple obedience be exalted beyond all worldly cleverness.

6. Then shall a pure and good conscience bring more joy than learned philosophy.

Then shall the contempt of riches far outweigh all the treasures of worldlings.

Then shall you find more comfort in having prayed devoutly than in having feasted daintily.

Then shall you rejoice more for having kept silence than for having talked much.

Then shall holy works be of greater value than many fair words.

Then shall strictness of life and hard penance please more than all the delights of earth.

---

[1] Mark ix, 43-49.
[2] Wisdom v, 1.
[3] 1 Corinthians iv, 10.
[4] Psalm cvi, 42.

Learn now to suffer in little things, that then you may be delivered from more grievous pains.

Try first here what you can endure hereafter.

If now you can endure so little, how will you be able to suffer eternal torments?

If now a little suffering makes you so impatient, what will hell-fire do hereafter?

Assuredly, you cannot have two heavens: this world's delights and the Kingdom of Christ hereafter.

7. Suppose that you have, to this very day, lived always in honours and pleasures; what would all that profit you, were you to die this moment?

All therefore is vanity,[1] except loving God and serving Him only.

For he that loves God with his whole heart, fears neither death, nor punishment, nor judgement, nor hell; for perfect love admits us surely to God.

But no wonder that the man who still delights in sin, should fear death and judgement.

However, if love cannot yet recall you from evil, it is good that the fear of hell at least should restrain you.

For, indeed, the man that lays aside the fear of God, will not be able to persevere in good, but will very soon fall into the snares of the devil.

CHAPTER 25

OF THE FERVENT AMENDMENT
OF OUR WHOLE LIFE

BE watchful and diligent in the service of God, and often reflect: What have I come here for,[2] and why have I left the world? Was it not that you might live for God and become a spiritual man?

Therefore, be keen to make progress; for soon shall you receive the reward of your labours. And then shall there be neither fear nor sorrow within your borders.

A little while shall you labour now; and presently you shall find great rest, yes, everlasting joy.

If you continue faithful and fervent in doing, God will surely be faithful and rich in rewarding.

You must keep a good and firm hope of coming to the

---

[1] Ecclesiastes i, 2.
[2] So St Bernard. See St Benedict's Rule, chap. 60.

crown; but you must not be over confident, lest you wax slothful or proud.

2. There was once a man of anxious mind, often wavering between hope and fear, who, overcome with sadness, threw himself upon the ground in prayer before one of the altars in the church, and revolving these things in his mind, said: O if I only knew that I should persevere! That very instant he heard within him this heavenly answer: And if you did know this, what would you do? Do now what you would then do, and you shall be perfectly secure.

And immediately, being consoled and comforted, he committed himself to the divine will, and his anxious wavering ceased.

He had no longer any desire to inquire curiously what should happen to him, but studied rather to learn what was the acceptable and perfect will of God,[1] for the beginning and the perfecting of every good work.

3. The Psalmist says: *Trust in the Lord, and do good, and dwell in the land, and you shall be fed with the riches thereof.*[2]

There is one thing that keeps many back from spiritual progress and from fervent amendment, namely, dread of the difficulty and the stress of the conflict.

Yet assuredly they especially do advance beyond others in virtue, who strive manfully to overcome those things which are hardest and most contrary to them.

For there does a man profit more and merit more abundant grace, where he more overcomes himself and mortifies his spirit.

4. All have not, indeed, equal difficulties to overcome and mortify. Yet a diligent and zealous person, though he have more passions, will make greater progress than another who is more docile but less fervent in the pursuit of virtues.

Two things especially conduce to great amendment, namely, forcibly to withdraw oneself from nature's vicious inclinations, and fervently to pursue the good that one most needs.

And take special care to shun and conquer those faults that commonly displease you in others.

5. Turn all occasions to your spiritual profit. If you see or hear of any good examples, be on fire to imitate them.

But, if you notice anything that is blameworthy, take care not to do the same thing yourself. Or, if you have ever done it, study to amend as soon as possible.

Even as your eye observes the conduct of others, even so are you in your turn observed by others.

[1] Romans xii, 2.
[2] Psalm xxxvi, 3.

How pleasant and sweet a thing it is, to see brethren who are fervent and devout, well-mannered and well-disciplined!

How sad and afflicting to see them walking disorderly, and not practising the things to which they are called!

How harmful a thing it is when they neglect the purpose of their vocation, and turn their minds to what is not their business!

6. Be mindful of the purpose you have undertaken, and place before you the image of the Crucified.

Well may you be ashamed, when looking upon the life of Jesus Christ, that as yet you have not studied more to conform yourself to Him, long as you have been in the way of God.

The religious who exercises himself earnestly and devoutly in the most holy life and passion of our Lord, shall find there abundantly all that is useful and necessary for him; nor need he go beyond Jesus, to seek something better.

O if Jesus crucified did but come into our hearts, how quickly and fully should we be instructed!

7. The fervent religious takes and bears well all things that are commanded him.

The negligent and lukewarm religious has trouble upon trouble, and endures anguish on every side; for he has no consolation within and is forbidden to seek it without.

The religious that lives not by discipline is exposed to dreadful ruin.

He that seeks what is easier and more lax will always be in trouble; for one thing or another will ever disgust him.

8. How do so many other religious manage, who live most strictly under the discipline of the cloister?

They seldom go abroad, they live retired, they are fed on the very poorest fare, they are coarsely clad, they labour much, they talk little, they keep long vigils, they rise early, they spend much time in prayer, they study frequently, and they keep themselves under strict discipline.

Consider the Carthusians, and the Cistercians, and the monks and nuns of other religious Orders, how they rise every night to sing praises to the Lord! And what a shame it would be for you to grow slothful in so holy a work, when so great a multitude of religious persons is already busy praising God!

9. O that there were nothing else to do but praise the Lord our God with our lips and with our whole heart! O that you did never need to eat, or drink, or sleep, but could always be praising God and occupied solely with spiritual pursuits! Then would you be much happier than now, when you are a slave to the body, on account of its manifold necessities.

Would to God that there were none of those necessities, but

only the banquets of the soul! But, alas! it is full seldom that we are able to taste of these.

10. When a man has arrived so far that he seeks his consolation from no created thing, then first does he begin to taste fully the sweetness of God. Then also will he be well content with whatever happens.

Then will he neither rejoice over great matters, nor be sorrowful for small, but commit himself wholly and trustfully to God, who is to him all in all. And, indeed, with God nothing perishes and nothing dies; for all things live unto Him and serve His merest nod with instant obedience.

11. Always remember your end, and consider that time lost returns no more.

Without care and diligence you shall never acquire virtues.

If once you begin to grow lukewarm, you begin to be in an evil condition.

But if you give yourself to fervour, you shall find great peace; and you shall feel your labour lighter, by the grace of God and the love of virtue.

The fervent and diligent man is ready for all things.

It is harder work to withstand our vices and passions than to toil at bodily labours.

He that does not shun small faults, falls little by little into greater.

You will always rejoice in the evening, if you spend the day profitably.

Watch over yourself, bestir yourself, admonish yourself, and, whatever may become of others, neglect not yourself.

In proportion as you do violence to yourself, so shall you make the greater progress. Amen.

THE SECOND BOOK

COUNSELS
CALLING TO THE INNER LIFE

CHAPTER 1

OF THE INNER LIFE

The Kingdom of God is within you,[1] says the Lord.
Turn to the Lord with your whole heart, and forsake this wretched world: your soul shall find rest.

Learn to despise outward things, and to give yourself to inward things: you shall see the Kingdom of God come within you.

The Kingdom of God is peace and joy in the Holy Ghost;[2] it is not given to the wicked.

Christ will come to you and discover His consolation to you, if you prepare Him a worthy dwelling within you.

All His glory and beauty are from within;[3] and there it is that He takes His delight.

Many are His visits to the man of inward life. With such a one He holds delightful converse, granting him sweet comfort, much peace, and an intimacy astonishing beyond measure.

2. Come then, faithful soul, prepare your heart for this your Spouse, so that He may vouchsafe to come to you and dwell within you.

For so He says: *If any man love Me, he will keep My word; and We will come to him and make Our dwelling with him.*[4]

Make room therefore for Christ, and refuse entrance to all others.

When you have Christ, you are rich and have need of nought else.

He will provide for you, and be in all things your faithful procurator; you shall not need to look to men.

For men soon change and quickly fail; but Christ abides for ever,[5] and stands by us steadily to the end.

[1] Luke xvii, 21.
[2] Romans xiv, 17.
[3] Psalm xliv, 14.
[4] John xiv, 23.
[5] John xii, 34.

3. We must not put any great trust in a frail and mortal man, useful and beloved though he be; nor should we be much grieved if he sometimes oppose and contradict us.

They that to-day are with you, to-morrow may be against you; for men often veer right round, like the wind.

Put your whole trust in God; let Him be your fear and your love.

He will answer for you, and will graciously do for you as shall be best.

You have no lasting city here.[1] Wherever you may be, you are a stranger and a pilgrim;[2] nor will you ever have rest, except you be inwardly united with Christ.

4. Why do you stand and look about you here, when this is not the place of your rest?

Your true dwelling is in heaven. As for all earthly things, you should give them no more than the look of a passer-by.

All things are passing away, and you too along with them.

See that you do not cling to them, lest you be caught and perish.

Let your meditation be on the Most High,[3] and your petitions directed to Christ without ceasing.

If you know not how to meditate on high and heavenly things, rest in the passion of Christ, and love to dwell within His sacred wounds.

For if you fly devoutly to the wounds of Jesus and the precious marks of His passion, you shall feel great strengthening in tribulation; nor will you much care for the slights of men, but will easily bear words of detraction.

5. Christ also in this world was despised by men, and in His greatest need was forsaken by His acquaintances and friends, and left to endure insults alone.

Christ chose to suffer and be despised; and do you dare to complain of any man?

Christ had enemies and detractors; and would you have all men for your friends and benefactors?

How shall your patience be crowned, if you meet with no adversity?

If you are unwilling to suffer contradiction, how shall you be the friend of Christ?

Suffer with Christ and for Christ, if you desire to reign with Christ.

6. Had you but once entered perfectly into the heart of Jesus, and tasted a little of His burning love, then would you care nothing for your own convenience or inconvenience, but

---

[1] Hebrews xiii. 14.
[2] Psalm xxxviii. 13.
[3] Wisdom v. 16.

would rather rejoice at the reproaches cast upon you; for the love of Jesus makes a man despise himself.

A lover of Jesus and of the truth, a truly inward man devoid of inordinate affections, can freely turn to God, transcend himself in spirit, and enjoy delightful rest.

7. He whose taste discerns all things as they are, and not as they are said or accounted to be, is truly a wise man, and taught rather by God than by men.

He that knows how to walk inwardly, and to make but little account of outward things, does not look for places, or wait for seasons, to perform his exercises of devotion.

The man of inward life soon recollects himself, because he never wholly surrenders himself to outward things.

Outward labour is no prejudice to him, nor any employment which for a time is necessary; but as things happen, so does he accommodate himself to them.

He who is well disposed and orderly within, cares not for the strange and perverse doings of men.

In proportion as a man draws things to himself, just so much is he hindered and distracted.

8. If all were right with you, and you were well purified from sin, everything would tend to your good and your profit.

The reason why many things displease you, and often disturb you, is this, that you are not yet perfectly dead to yourself, nor detached from all earthly things.

There is nothing that so defiles and entangles the heart of man as the impure love of creatures.

If you refuse outward consolations, then you will be able to apply your mind to heavenly things, and frequently to experience inward joy.

CHAPTER 2

OF HUMBLE SUBMISSION

MAKE no great account of what man is for you or against you, but mind and take care of this, that God be with you in everything you do.

Have a good conscience, and God shall well defend you; for no man's malice can hurt him whom God wills to help.

If you know how to be silent and to suffer, you shall without doubt see the help of the Lord.

He Himself knows the time and the manner of your deliverance; and therefore it is your part to resign yourself into His hands.

It belongs to God to help us and deliver us from all trouble.

Many a time it is of much advantage towards keeping us in greater humility that others know and rebuke our faults.

2. When a man humbles himself for his faults, then he readily pacifies others, and easily satisfies those who are angry with him.

God protects the humble man and delivers him; the humble He loves and consoles; to the humble He inclines Himself; on the humble He bestows abundant grace; and, after he has been brought low, He raises him up to glory.

To the humble man He reveals His secrets, and sweetly draws and invites him to Himself.

The humble man, though he suffer shame, remains in great peace; for he relies upon God and not upon the world.

Never think that you have made any progress, unless you esteem yourself inferior to all.

CHAPTER 3

OF THE GOOD PEACEABLE MAN

FIRST keep yourself in peace, and then shall you be able to bring others to peace.

The peaceable man does more good than one that is very learned.

The passionate man turns even good to evil, and readily believes evil. But the good peaceable man turns all things to good.

He that is in perfect peace suspects no man. But he that is discontented and troubled is agitated by various suspicions; he neither has rest himself, nor suffers others to rest.

Many a time he says what he ought not to say, and leaves undone what it were better for him to do.

He considers what others ought to do, and neglects what he is bound to do himself.

Therefore, be zealous first of all regarding yourself, and then may you justly exercise zeal towards your neighbour also.

2. You know well how to excuse and gloss over your own deeds, but you are not willing to accept the excuses of others.

It were more just for you to accuse yourself and excuse your brother.

If you wish to be borne with, bear also with others.

See how far you are as yet from true charity and humility; for he that has these cannot feel anger or indignation against any one but himself.

It is no great thing to associate with the good and the gentle, for this is naturally pleasing to all men. Every one prefers peace, and loves those best that agree with him.

But to be able to live peacefully with the difficult and the perverse, or with the undisciplined and those that contradict us, this is a great grace, and a thing highly commendable and manly.

3. Some there are who keep themselves in peace, and have peace also with others. And there are some who neither have peace themselves, nor leave others in peace; they are troublesome to others, and still more troublesome to themselves.

And there are those who keep themselves in peace, and study to bring others to peace.

Nevertheless, all our peace in this wretched life must be placed rather in humble endurance than in the absence of contradiction.

He who best knows how to suffer will possess the greater peace.

Such a one is conqueror of himself and lord of the world, the friend of Christ and heir of heaven.

CHAPTER 4

OF A PURE MIND AND A SIMPLE INTENTION

By two wings is a man lifted above earthly things, namely, by simplicity and purity.

Simplicity must be in the intention, purity in the affection. Simplicity aims at God, purity apprehends Him and tastes Him.

No good work will be a hindrance to you, if you be inwardly free from inordinate affection.

If you aim at and seek nothing else but the will of God and your neighbour's benefit, then shall you enjoy inward liberty.

If only your heart were right, then every created thing would be to you a mirror of life and a book of holy teaching.

There is no creature so little and so vile as not to manifest the goodness of God.

2. If you were inwardly good and pure, then would you discern all things without impediment, and comprehend them aright. A pure heart penetrates heaven and hell.

According as every one is inwardly, so does he judge outwardly.

If there be joy in the world, truly the man of pure heart possesses it.

And if there be anywhere tribulation and distress, an evil conscience does the more readily experience it.

As iron cast into the fire loses its rust and becomes all white with the heat, so the man that turns himself wholly to God is divested of all sloth and changed into a new man.

3. When a man begins to grow lukewarm, then he is afraid of a little labour, and willingly receives outward consolation.

But when he begins perfectly to overcome himself, and to walk manfully in the way of God, then he makes little account of things that formerly seemed to him grievous.

CHAPTER 5

OF SELF-CONSIDERATION

WE must not trust too much to ourselves; for grace and understanding are often wanting to us. There is in us but little light, and this we soon lose by negligence.

Often too we are quite unconscious how inwardly blind we are.

We often do amiss, and then do worse by excusing ourselves.

Sometimes we are moved by passion, and think it zeal.

We blame little things in others, and overlook great things in ourselves.

We are quick enough in perceiving and weighing what we bear from others; but we give little thought to what others have to bear from us.

He that should well and justly weigh his own doings would find little cause to judge harshly of another.

2. The truly inward man puts the care of himself before all other cares; and he that looks diligently to himself finds it easy to be silent about others.

You will never be spiritual and devout, unless you pass over in silence other men's concerns and look especially to yourself.

If you attend wholly to yourself and to God, what you see abroad will affect you but little.

Where are you when you are not present to yourself?

And when you have surveyed the whole world, what good has it done you if you have neglected yourself?

If you would have true peace and perfect union, you must cast all things else aside and keep your eyes upon yourself alone.

3. Then will you make great progress, when you keep yourself free from every temporal anxiety.

You will fall back exceedingly, if you make account of anything temporal.

Let there be nothing great, nothing high, nothing pleasant, nothing acceptable to you but only God Himself, or what comes from God.

Think it all vanity, whatever consolation you may meet with from any creature.

The soul that loves God despises all things that are less than God.

God only, the eternal and infinite, who fills all things, is the soul's solace and the true joy of the heart.

CHAPTER 6

OF THE JOY OF A GOOD CONSCIENCE

THE glory of a good man is the testimony of a good conscience.[1]

Have a good conscience and you shall always have joy.

A good conscience can bear very much, and is very joyful in the midst of adversity.

But an evil conscience is always fearful and uneasy. Sweetly shall you rest, if your heart do not blame you.

Never rejoice, except when you have done well.

The wicked never have true joy, nor feel inward peace; because (says the Lord) *there is no peace for the wicked.*[2]

And if they say: We are in peace, and there shall no evil come upon us, and who is there shall dare to harm us?[3] believe them not; for suddenly the anger of God shall arise, and their deeds shall be brought to nothing, and their thoughts shall perish.

2. To glory in tribulation is not hard for him that loves; for to glory so is to glory in the cross of the Lord.

Short-lived is the glory that is given and received by men.

The glory of this world is always attended by sorrow.

The glory of the good is in their own consciences and not in the mouths of men.

The joy of the just is from God and in God, and their rejoicing is in the truth.

He that longs after true and everlasting glory, cares not for that which is temporal.

And he that seeks temporal glory, or does not from his heart despise it, shows himself to have little love for the glory of heaven.

[1] 2 Corinthians i, 12.
[2] Isaias xlviii, 22.
[3] Micheas iii, 11.

He has great tranquillity of heart who cares nothing for praise or blame.

3. He will easily be contented and at peace whose conscience is clean.

You are not more holy for being praised, nor worse for being blamed.

What you are, that you are; nor can words make you greater than you are in God's sight.

If you consider what you are inwardly, you will not care what men say of you.

Man looks on the face, but God sees into the heart.

Man considers the actions, but God weighs the intentions.

Always to do well, and to esteem oneself of small account, is the mark of a humble soul.

To refuse consolation from any creature is a sign of great purity and of inward confidence.

4. He that seeks no outward testimony for himself, shows plainly that he has committed himself wholly to God.

For Saint Paul says: *Not he that commends himself is approved, but he whom God commends.*[1]

To walk within with God, and to be bound by no outward affection: this is the state of the truly inward man.

CHAPTER 7

OF THE LOVE OF JESUS ABOVE ALL THINGS

BLESSED is he that understands what it is to love Jesus, and to despise himself for the sake of Jesus.

We must quit what is beloved for the sake of the Beloved; for Jesus will be loved alone and above all things.

The love of things created is deceitful and inconstant; the love of Jesus is faithful and enduring.

He that clings to the creature shall fall with its falling.

He that embraces Jesus shall stand firm for ever.

Love Him, and keep Him for your friend, who, when all go away, will not forsake you, nor suffer you to perish finally.

Sooner or later you must be separated from all, whether you will or no.

2. In life and in death keep yourself near to Jesus, and entrust yourself to His fidelity, who alone can help you when all others fail.

The nature of your Beloved is such that He will not admit

[1] 2 Corinthians x, 18.

of a rival; He will have your heart for Himself alone, and sit as King upon His own throne.

If you could empty your heart of every creature, Jesus would willingly make His dwelling with you.

Whatsoever reliance you place in men apart from Jesus, you will find to be wellnigh lost.

Trust not nor lean upon a reed shaken by the wind.

For all flesh is grass, and all the glory thereof shall fade like the flower of grass.[1]

3. You will soon be deceived, if you regard only the outward appearance of men. Indeed, if you seek in others your comfort and your profit, you will too often meet with loss.

If in all things you seek Jesus, truly you shall find Jesus; if you seek yourself, you shall find yourself also, but to your own ruin.

For if a man does not seek Jesus, he does himself more harm than the whole world and all his enemies can do him.

CHAPTER 8

OF FAMILIAR FRIENDSHIP
WITH JESUS

WHEN Jesus is present, all is well, and nothing seems difficult; but when Jesus is absent, everything is hard.

When Jesus does not speak within, consolation is little worth; but if Jesus speak but one word, we feel great consolation.

Did not Mary Magdalen instantly rise up from the place where she wept, when Martha said to her : *The Master is here, and calls for thee*?[2]

Happy hour! when Jesus calls from tears to spiritual joy.

How dry and hard are you without Jesus! How foolish and vain, if you desire anything besides Jesus!

Is not this a greater loss than if you should lose the whole world?

2. What can the world give you without Jesus?

To be without Jesus is a grievous hell; to be with Jesus a sweet paradise.

If Jesus be with you, no foe can harm you.

Whoever finds Jesus finds a good treasure, yes, a good above every good.

[1] Isaias xl, 6.
[2] John xi, 28.

And he that loses Jesus loses a very great deal, more even than the whole world.

He that lives without Jesus is in wretched poverty; and he who is familiar with Jesus is exceeding rich.

3. It is a great art to know how to converse with Jesus; and to know how to keep Jesus is great wisdom.

Be humble and peaceable, and Jesus will be with you. Be devout and calm, and Jesus will abide with you.

You may soon drive away Jesus and lose His grace, if you turn aside after outward things.

And if you drive Him from you and lose Him, to whom will you fly? and whom, then, will you seek for your friend?

Without a friend, you cannot live well; and if Jesus be not your friend above all other friends, you shall indeed be sad and desolate.

You do foolishly, therefore, to trust in any other, or to rejoice in any other.

We ought rather to choose to have the whole world against us than to offend Jesus.

Of all, therefore, that are dear to you, let Jesus alone be your special beloved.

4. Let all be loved for the sake of Jesus, but Jesus for His own sake.

Jesus Christ alone is singly to be loved; for He alone is found good and faithful above all friends.

For His sake, and in Him, let enemies as well as friends be dear to you; and for all these you must pray to Him, that all may know and love Him.

Never desire to be singularly praised or loved; for this belongs to God alone, who has none like to Himself.

Neither desire that any one's heart should be taken up with you; nor be you much taken up with the love of any one; but let Jesus be in you, and in every good man.

5. Be pure and free inwardly, and be not entangled by any creature.

You must be naked, and bear a pure heart towards God, if you would be at peace and see how sweet is the Lord.[1]

And this, of a truth, you shall not attain unless you be forestalled and drawn by His grace. But then, having cast out and dismissed all else, you shall be united to Him, alone with the Alone.

For when the grace of God comes to a man, then is he able for all things; and when it departs, then is he poor and weak, and left only as it were to be flogged.

[1] Psalm xxxiii, 9.

Yet he must not then be dejected, nor despair; but wait calmly upon the will of God, and for the honour of Jesus Christ endure whatever may befall him. For after winter follows summer; after night the day returns; after the storm comes a great calm.

CHAPTER 9

OF THE WANT OF ALL CONSOLATION

IT is not hard to despise all human consolation when we have divine.

But it is a great thing, yes, a very great thing, to be able to forgo all comfort, both human and divine, and to be willing to bear this heart's exile for God's honour, and seek oneself in nothing, nor regard one's own deserts.

What great thing is it, if you be cheerful and devout when grace comes? This hour is desired by all men.

He rides very pleasantly who is carried by the grace of God.

And what wonder if he feel no burden, who is borne up by the Almighty, and led by the Sovereign Guide?

2. We love to have something to comfort us, and it is hard for a man to divest himself of self-love.

The holy Martyr Laurence, with his priest, overcame the world, because he despised whatever seemed delightful in this world. And, for the love of Christ, he even patiently suffered God's high priest, Sixtus, whom he loved exceedingly, to be taken away from him.

So he overcame the love of man by the love of the Creator; and instead of human consolation he made choice rather of God's good pleasure.

Even so must you also learn to part with an intimate and beloved friend for the love of God.

Take it not to heart when you are forsaken by a friend, knowing that at the last we must all be parted one from another.

3. A man will have a great and long struggle with himself, before he fully learns to master self and to turn his whole affection towards God.

When a man relies on himself, he easily turns aside to human consolations.

But a true lover of Christ, and a diligent pursuer of virtue, does not fall back upon consolations, nor seek such sensible sweetnesses; he prefers hard trials and would wish to undergo severe labours for Christ.

4. Therefore, when God gives spiritual consolation, receive it with thanksgiving; but know that it is God's gift, and not any desert of your own.

Be not puffed up, nor overjoyed, nor vainly presumptuous; but rather be the more humble for the gift, more cautious too and fearful in all your actions; for that hour will pass away, and temptation will follow.

When consolation shall be taken away from you, do not presently despair; but with humility and patience await the heavenly visitation; for God is able to give you again more abundant consolation.

This is nothing new or strange to those who have experience of God's ways; for among the great Saints and ancient Prophets there was often the same kind of alternation.

5. Hence there was one who, when grace was with him, exclaimed : *I said in my prosperity, I shall not be moved for ever.*[1]

But when grace was withdrawn, he tells us what he experienced in himself : *Thou didst turn away Thy face from me, and I was troubled.*[2]

Yet even then he does not despair at all, but more earnestly beseeches the Lord, and says : *Unto Thee, O Lord, will I cry; and unto my God will I make supplication.*[3]

At length he received the fruit of his prayer, and testifies that he was heard, saying : *The Lord has heard, and has had pity on me; the Lord is become my helper.*[4]

But in what way? *Thou hast turned,* he says, *my mourning into joy, and thou hast encompassed me with gladness.*[5]

If it has been thus with great Saints, we that are weak and poor must not be discouraged if we are sometimes fervent, sometimes cold; for the Spirit comes and goes according to His own good pleasure.[6]

Wherefore holy Job says : *Thou dost visit him early in the morning, and on a sudden Thou triest him.*[7]

6. Wherein then can I hope, or in what must I put my trust, but in God's great mercy alone, and in the sole hope of heavenly grace?

For whether I have by me good men, or devout brethren, or faithful friends, or holy books, or beautiful treatises, or sweet canticles and hymns: all these help but little, and have

[1] Psalm xxix, 7.
[2] *Ibid.*, 8.
[3] *Ibid.*, 9.
[4] *Ibid.*, 11.
[5] *Ibid.*, 12.
[6] John iii, 8.
[7] Job vii, 18.

but little savour, when I am forsaken by grace, and left in my own poverty.

At such a time there is no better remedy than patience and self-denial, in full accordance with the will of God.

7. I never found any one so religious and devout as not sometimes to experience a withdrawal of grace, or feel a lessening of fervour.

No Saint was ever so sublimely rapt and illuminated as not to be tempted sooner or later.

For he is not worthy of the sublime contemplation of God, who has not for God's sake been exercised with some tribulation.

And when temptation goes before, it is usually a sign that consolation will follow.

For heavenly comfort is promised to such as have been proved by temptation.

The Lord says : *To him that shall overcome, I will give to eat of the tree of life.* [1]

8. Now divine consolation is given that a man may bear adversities more stoutly. And temptation follows, lest he grow proud for the good gift.

The devil sleeps not, neither is the flesh yet dead; therefore you must not cease to prepare yourself for the battle; for on the right hand and on the left are enemies that never rest.

CHAPTER 10

OF GRATITUDE FOR THE GRACE
OF GOD

WHY do you look for rest, when you were born for labour?

Dispose yourself to patience, rather than to consolations; and to carrying the cross, rather than to gladness.

For what secular is there that would not willingly receive consolation and spiritual joy, if he could obtain it at all times?

Spiritual consolations, indeed, surpass all the delights of the world and all the pleasures of the flesh.

For all worldly delights are either vain or impure; but spiritual delights alone are delightful and honourable. They spring from virtue, and are infused by God into minds that are pure.

But no man can always enjoy these divine consolations when he will, because the time of temptation is not long absent.

[1] Apocalypse ii, 7.

2. But false liberty of mind and much self-confidence are a great hindrance to the heavenly visitation.

God does well in giving the grace of consolation; but man does ill in not returning all again to God with thanksgiving.

And this is the reason why the gifts of grace cannot flow in us : that we are ungrateful to the Giver and do not return all to the Source.

For grace will always be given to him that duly returns thanks; and what is wont to be given to the humble, shall be taken away from the proud.

3. I would not have any such consolation as robs me of compunction; nor do I wish to have such contemplation as leads to pride.

For all that is high is not holy; nor is every pleasant thing good, nor every desire pure; nor is everything that is dear to us pleasing to God.

I willingly accept of that grace which always makes me more humble and fearful and more ready to renounce myself.

He that has been taught by the gift of grace, and instructed by the chastisement of its withdrawal, will not dare to attribute anything of good to himself, but will rather acknowledge himself to be poor and naked.

Give to God what is God's, and ascribe to yourself what is yours; that is, give thanks to God for His grace; but, as to yourself, know that nothing is to be attributed to you but sin, and the punishment due to sin.

4. Put yourself always in the lowest place, and the highest shall be given you; for the highest cannot be without the lowest.

The Saints that are the highest in the sight of God are the least in their own eyes; and the more glorious they are, the more humble are they in themselves.

Full of truth and the glory of heaven, they have no desire for empty glory. Being grounded and established in God, they can by no means be proud.

And when men attribute to God whatsoever good they have received, they seek no glory from one another, but only that glory which is from God; and they desire above all things that God may be praised in Himself and in all the Saints, and for that they are ever striving.

5. Be grateful, then, for the least gift, and you shall be worthy to receive greater gifts.

Let the least be to you as something very great, and the meanest seem a special favour.

If you consider the dignity of the Giver, no gift will seem

little or too mean for you. For that is not little which is given by the most high God.

Yes, though he give punishment and stripes, it ought to be welcome to you; for, whatever He suffers to befall us, it is always done for our salvation.

He that desires to retain the grace of God, let him be thankful for grace when it is given, and patient when it is withdrawn.

Let him pray that it may return; let him be wary and humble, lest he lose it.

CHAPTER 11

HOW FEW ARE THE LOVERS OF THE CROSS OF JESUS

JESUS has now many lovers of His heavenly kingdom, but few bearers of His cross.

He has many that are desirous of consolation, but few of tribulation.

He finds many companions of His table, but few of His abstinence.

All desire to rejoice with Him, but few are willing to endure anything for His sake.

Many follow Jesus to the breaking of bread, but few to the drinking of the chalice of His passion.

Many reverence His miracles, but few follow the shame of His cross.

Many love Jesus as long as they meet with no adversity; many praise Him and bless Him as long as they receive some consolations from Him.

But if Jesus hide Himself and leave them for a little while, they either murmur or fall into excessive dejection.

2. But, if men love Jesus for Jesus' sake, and not for the sake of some consolation of their own, they bless Him no less in tribulation and anguish of heart than in the greatest consolation.

And though He should never give them consolation, yet would they always praise Him, and always give Him thanks.

3. O how powerful is the pure love of Jesus, when mixed with no self-interest or self-love!

Are not all they to be called hirelings who are ever seeking consolations?

Do they not prove themselves to be rather lovers of themselves than of Christ, who are always thinking of their own advantage and gain?

Where shall we find a man that is willing to serve God without seeking reward?

4. Seldom do we find any one so spiritual as to be stripped of all things.

For who shall find a man that is truly poor in spirit and detached from all created things? *From afar and from the uttermost coasts is his price.*[1]

If a man give his whole substance,[2] still it is nothing.

And if he do great penance, it is but little.

And if he attain to all knowledge, he is far off still.

And if he have great virtue and very fervent devotion, there is still much wanting to him, namely, the one thing which is supremely necessary for him.

What is that? That having left all things else, he leave also himself, and wholly go out of himself, and retain nothing of self-love.

And when he shall have done all things which he knows he ought to do, let him think that he has done nothing.

5. Let him not make great account of that which might be much esteemed; but let him in truth acknowledge himself to be an unprofitable servant. For the Truth says: *When you shall have done all things that have been commanded you, say, We are unprofitable servants.*[3]

Then may he be truly poor in spirit, and may say with the Psalmist: *I am alone and poor.*[4]

Yet no man is richer, no man more powerful, no man more free than he who knows how to leave himself and all things, and to put himself in the very lowest place.

CHAPTER 12

OF THE ROYAL ROAD OF
THE HOLY CROSS

To many this seems a hard saying: *Deny yourself, take up your cross, and follow Jesus.*[5]

But it will be much harder to hear that last word: *Depart from Me, ye cursed, into everlasting fire.*[6]

For they who now love to hear and follow the word of the

---

[1] Proverbs xxxi, 10.
[2] Canticle of Canticles viii, 7.
[3] Luke xvii, 10.
[4] Psalm xxiv, 16.
[5] Matthew xvi, 24.
[6] *Ibid.*, xxv, 41.

cross, shall not then fear to hear the sentence of eternal damnation.

This sign of the cross shall be in heaven when the Lord shall come to judgement.

Then all the servants of the cross, who in their lifetime have conformed themselves to Christ crucified, shall come before Christ their Judge with great confidence.

2. Why, then, are you afraid to take up your cross, which leads to the Kingdom?

In the cross is salvation; in the cross is life; in the cross is protection from enemies.

In the cross is infusion of heavenly sweetness; in the cross is strength of mind; in the cross is joy of spirit.

In the cross is height of virtue; in the cross is perfection of sanctity.

There is no health of soul, nor hope of eternal life, but in the cross.

Take up, therefore, your cross, and follow Jesus, and you shall go into life everlasting.

He is gone before you carrying His cross, and He died for you upon the cross, that you also may bear your cross, and love to die on the cross.

Because if you die with Him, you shall also live with Him; and if you are His companion in suffering, you shall be His companion also in glory.

3. Lo, in the cross does all consist, and all lies in our dying; and there is no other way to life and to true interior peace, but the way of the holy cross and of daily mortification.

Go where you will, seek what you will, you shall not find a higher way above, nor a safer way below, than the way of the holy cross.

Dispose and order all things according as you will, and as seems best to you; and you will still find something to suffer, either willingly or unwillingly; and so you shall always find the cross.

For either you shall feel pain in the body, or else you shall suffer tribulation of soul.

4. Sometimes you shall be deserted by God; at other times you shall be afflicted by your neighbour; and, what is more, you shall often be a trouble to yourself.

Neither can you be delivered or eased by any remedy or comfort; but as long as it shall please God, so long must you bear it.

For God wills that you learn to suffer tribulation without comfort, and that you wholly submit yourself to Him, and by tribulation become more humble.

No man has so heartfelt a sense of the passion of Christ as he whose lot it has been to suffer like things.

The cross, therefore, is always ready, and everywhere awaits you.

You cannot escape it, whithersoever you run. For wheresoever you go you carry yourself with you, and shall always find yourself.

Turn upwards, or turn downwards; turn inwards, or turn outwards: everywhere you shall find the cross.

And everywhere you must of necessity hold fast to patience, if you desire inward peace and would merit an everlasting crown.

5. If you carry the cross willingly, it will carry you, and bring you to your desired end, namely, to that place where there will be an end of suffering, though here there shall be no end.

If you carry it unwillingly, you make it a burden to you, and load yourself the more, and nevertheless you must bear it.

If you fling away one cross, without doubt you will find another, and perhaps a heavier.

6. Do you think to escape that which no mortal ever could avoid? What Saint ever was in the world without the cross and tribulation?

For even our Lord Jesus Christ Himself was not for one hour of His life without the anguish of His passion.

It behoved, said He, *that Christ should suffer, and rise from the dead, and so enter into His glory.*[1]

And why do you seek another way than this royal way, which is the way of the holy cross?

The whole life of Christ was a cross and a martyrdom, and do you seek for yourself rest and joy?

7. You err, you err, if you seek anything else than to suffer tribulation; for this whole mortal life is full of miseries, and everywhere marked with crosses.

And the higher a person is advanced in spirit, the heavier crosses shall he often meet with; because the pain of his banishment increases in proportion to his love.

Yet such a one, thus many ways afflicted, is not without some relief of consolation; because he is sensible of the very great profit he reaps by bearing his cross.

8. For whilst he willingly resigns himself to it, all the burden of tribulation is converted into an assured hope of divine consolation.

And the more the flesh is brought down by affliction, so much the more is the spirit strengthened by interior grace.

---

[1] Luke xxiv, 26, 46.

And sometimes he gains such strength through affection to tribulation and adversity, by his love of conformity to the cross of Christ, that he is not willing to be without suffering and tribulation; because such a one believes himself to be so much the more acceptable to God, the more and more grievous things he shall be able to bear for His sake.

This is not the power of man, but the grace of Christ; which can and does effect such great things in frail flesh, that what it naturally abhors and flies, even this, through fervour of spirit, it now embraces and loves.

9. To bear the cross; to love the cross; to chastise the body and bring it under subjection; to fly honours; to love to suffer insults; to despise oneself, and to wish to be despised; to bear all adversities and losses, and to desire no prosperity in this world: none of this is according to man's natural inclination,

If you rely upon yourself, you can of your own power do nothing of this sort.

But if you trust in the Lord, strength shall be given you from heaven, and the world and the flesh shall be made subject to you.

Neither shall you fear even your enemy the devil, if you be armed with faith, and signed with the cross of Christ.

10. Set yourself, then, like a good and faithful servant of Christ, to bear manfully the cross of your Lord, who for love of you was crucified.

Prepare yourself to suffer many adversities and various evils in this miserable life; for so it will be with you, wherever you are, and so indeed will you find it, wheresoever you hide yourself.

It must be so; and there is no way of escape from tribulation and sorrow other than patient endurance.

Drink of the chalice of your Lord lovingly, if you desire to be His friend and to have part with Him.

Leave consolations to God, to do with them as best pleases Him.

But be ready on your part to bear tribulations, and see that you account them the greatest consolations. For, although you alone could suffer them all, the sufferings of this life are not worthy to be compared with the glory to come,[1] that is to be earned by them.

11. When you shall arrive thus far that tribulation shall be sweet to you, and you shall relish it for the love of Christ, then think that it is well with you, for you have found a paradise upon earth.

As long as suffering is grievous to you and you seek to fly

[1] Romans viii, 18.

from it, so long shall it be ill with you; and the desire of flying from tribulation shall pursue you everywhere.

12. If you set yourself to what you ought, that is to suffer and to die, it will quickly be better with you, and you shall find peace.

Although you should have been rapt to the third heaven with St. Paul, you are not thereby secured that you shall suffer no adversity. For Jesus said : *I will show him how great things he must suffer for My name's sake.*[1]

To suffer, therefore, is what awaits you, if you are resolved to love Jesus, and constantly to serve Him.

13. Would to God you were worthy to suffer something for the name of Jesus! How great glory would remain for yourself, how great joy would it be to all the Saints of God, and how great also the edification to your neighbour!

All men recommend patience; but few are they that are willing to suffer.

With good reason ought you willingly to suffer a little for Christ, since many suffer greater things for the world.

14. Know for certain that you must lead a dying life; for the more a man dies to himself, the more does he begin to live to God.

No man is fit to comprehend heavenly things, who has not resigned himself to suffer adversities for Christ.

Nothing is more acceptable to God, nothing more salutary for you in this world, than to suffer willingly for Christ.

And, if you had the choice, you ought to prefer to suffer adversities for Christ, than to be refreshed with many consolations; because then you would more resemble Christ, and be more likened to all the Saints.

For our merit and our spiritual progress do not consist in having many sweetnesses and consolations, but rather in bearing great afflictions and tribulations.

15. If, indeed, there had been anything better and more beneficial to man's salvation than suffering, Christ certainly would have shown it by word and example.

But He manifestly exhorts both His disciples that followed Him, and all that desire to follow Him, to bear the cross, saying: *If any man will come after Me, let him deny himself, and take up his cross, and follow Me.*[2]

Therefore, when we have read to the end and searched through all, let this be the final conclusion, that *through many tribulations must we enter into the Kingdom of God.*[3]

---

[1] Acts ix, 16.
[2] Luke ix, 23.
[3] Acts xiv, 22.

THE THIRD BOOK

OF INWARD CONSOLATION

CHAPTER 1

HOW CHRIST SPEAKS INWARDLY TO
A FAITHFUL SOUL

I WILL *hear what the Lord God speaks within me.*[1] Blessed is the soul that hears the Lord speaking within her, and receives from His mouth the word of consolation.

Blessed the ears that catch the pulses of the divine whisper,[2] and take no notice of the whisperings of this world.

Blessed, indeed, are those ears that do not listen to the voice which sounds without, but attend to Truth itself teaching within.

Blessed the eyes that are shut to outward things but intent on inward things.

Blessed are they that penetrate into those inward things, and by daily exercises strive to make themselves more and more fit for the reception of heavenly secrets.

Blessed are they that rejoice to be occupied wholly with God, and that shake off every worldly impediment.

2. Consider these things, O my soul, and shut the doors of your sensual desires, so that you may hear what the Lord God speaks within you.

Thus says your Beloved: I am your salvation,[3] your peace, and your life.

Keep yourself with Me, and you shall find peace.

Let go all transitory things; seek the eternal. What are all temporal things but seductive snares? And what good are all creatures, if you be forsaken by the Creator?

Therefore, cast off all earthly things and make yourself pleasing to your Creator, that so you may attain true happiness.

[1] Psalm lxxxiv, 9.
[2] Job iv, 12.
[3] Psalm xxxiv, 3.

CHAPTER 2

THAT TRUTH SPEAKS WITHIN US
WITHOUT NOISE OF WORDS

SPEAK, *Lord, for Thy servant heareth.*[1] *I am Thy servant; give me understanding, that I may know Thy testimonies.*[2]

Incline my heart to the words of Thy mouth;[3] let Thy speech distil as the dew.[4]

Formerly the children of Israel said to Moses : *Speak thou to us, and we will hear; let not the Lord speak to us, lest we die.*[5]

Not thus, O Lord, not thus do I pray; but rather with the Prophet Samuel I humbly and earnestly entreat: *Speak, Lord, for Thy servant heareth.*

Let not Moses, nor any of the Prophets, speak to me: speak Thou rather, O Lord God, the Inspirer and Enlightener of all the Prophets; for Thou alone, without them, canst perfectly instruct me; but they, without Thee, will avail me nothing.

2. They may indeed sound forth words, but they give not the spirit.

Beautifully do they speak; but if Thou be silent, they kindle not the heart.

They give the letter, but Thou dost disclose the spirit.

They announce mysteries, but Thou dost unlock their secret meaning.

They declare the commandments, but Thou dost enable us to fulfil them.

They point out the way, but Thou givest strength to walk in it.

They work outwardly only, but Thou dost instruct and enlighten the heart.

They water without, but Thou givest the increase.

They cry aloud in words, but Thou dost impart understanding to the hearing.

3. So let not Moses speak to me; but do Thou speak, O Lord my God, the eternal Truth, lest I die and prove fruitless, if I be admonished outwardly only, and not enkindled within; lest I be condemned at the Judgement because the word was heard

[1] 1 Kings iii, 10.
[2] Psalm cxviii, 125.
[3] Psalm lxxvii, 1.
[4] Deuteronomy xxxii, 2.
[5] Exodus xx, 19.

and not fulfilled, known and not loved, believed and not observed.

Speak, then, Lord, for Thy servant heareth; for Thou hast the words of eternal life.[1]

Speak Thou to me, that it may bring comfort to my soul and the amendment of my whole life, and redound also to Thy praise, and glory, and everlasting honour.

CHAPTER 3

THAT THE WORDS OF GOD ARE TO BE HEARD WITH HUMILITY, AND THAT MANY WEIGH THEM NOT

MY son, hear My words, words most sweet, excelling all the learning of philosophers and the wise men of this world.

My words are spirit and life,[2] and are not to be weighed by human standards.

They are not to be abused for empty delight, but to be heard in silence and received with all humility and great affection.

And I said: *Blessed is the man whom Thou, O Lord, shalt instruct, and shalt teach out of Thy Law; that Thou mayest give him rest from the evil days,*[3] and that he may not be desolate upon the earth.

I (says the Lord) have taught the Prophets from the beginning, and even till now I cease not to speak to all. But many are deaf and hardened to My voice.

2. Many listen more willingly to the world than to God, and are readier to follow the desires of their flesh than God's good pleasure.

The world promises things temporal and of small value, and is served with great eagerness; I promise things most excellent and everlasting, and yet men's hearts remain sluggish.

Who is there that serves and obeys Me in all things with that great care with which the world and its lords are served? *Be ashamed, O Sidon, says the sea.*[4]

And if you ask the reason, here it is.

For a scanty competence, men run a great way; for eternal life, many will scarce lift a foot once from the ground.

A petty gain is sought after; for a single coin men sometimes

[1] John vi, 68.
[2] *Ibid.*, 63.
[3] Psalm xciii, 12, 13.
[4] Isaias xxiii, 4.

go shamefully to law; for some mere trifle or a slight promise men will brave toil day and night.

3. But, the shame of it! for an unchangeable good, for an inestimable reward, for the highest honour and never-ending glory, they are loth to undergo even a little fatigue.

Blush, then, slothful and querulous servant, that they are actually more ready to labour for death than you for life.

They rejoice more in vanity than you do in the truth.

Sometimes, indeed, they are disappointed of their hopes; but My promise deceives no man, nor sends away empty him that trusts in Me.

What I have promised, I will give; what I have said, I will make good; if only a man continue to the end faithful in My love.

I am the Rewarder of all the good, and the mighty Prover of all the devout.

4. Write My words in your heart, and think diligently on them; for they will be very necessary in the time of temptation.

What you understand not when you read, you shall know in the day of visitation.

I am accustomed to visit My elect in two ways, namely, with temptation and with consolation.

And I daily read two lessons to them: one to rebuke their vices, the other to exhort them to the increase of virtue.

He that has My words and slights them, has One who shall judge him at the last day.[1]

A PRAYER
TO IMPLORE THE GRACE OF DEVOTION

5. O Lord my God, Thou art all my good; and who am I, that I should dare to speak to Thee?

I am Thy most poor servant, and a wretched little worm, much more poor and contemptible than I can conceive, or dare express.

Yet remember, O Lord, that I am nothing, that I have nothing, and can do nothing.

Thou alone art good, just, and holy; Thou canst do all things; Thou givest all things; Thou fillest all things, leaving only the sinner empty.

Remember Thy tender mercies,[2] and fill my heart with Thy grace, Thou who wilt not that Thy works should be void.

6. How can I endure myself in this wretched life, unless Thy mercy and grace strengthen me?

[1] John xii, 48.
[2] Psalm xxiv, 6.

Turn not away Thy face from me, delay not Thy visitation, withdraw not Thy consolation, lest my soul become to Thee as a land without water.

O Lord, teach me to do Thy will; teach me to live worthily and humbly in Thy sight; for Thou art my wisdom; Thou knowest me in the Truth, and didst know me before the world was made, and before I was born in the world.

CHAPTER 4

THAT WE OUGHT TO WALK BEFORE GOD IN TRUTH AND HUMILITY

My son, walk before Me in truth; and seek Me always in the simplicity of your heart.

He that walks before Me in truth shall be secure against the assaults of evil. The truth shall deliver him from seducers and from the detractions of the wicked.

If the truth shall have made you free, you shall be free indeed,[1] and shall make no account of the vain words of men.

True, O Lord; and as Thou sayest, I beseech Thee, so let it be done to me. Let Thy truth teach me, let it guard me and preserve me to final salvation.

Let it deliver me from all evil affection and inordinate love, and I shall walk with Thee in great liberty of heart.

2. I will teach you (says the Truth) those things that are right and pleasing in My sight.

Think on your sins with great displeasure and sorrow; and never esteem yourself to be anything on account of your good works.

Of a truth you are a sinner, subject to, and entangled with, many passions.

Of yourself you always tend to nothing, speedily do you fail, speedily are you overcome, speedily disturbed, speedily dissipated.

You have nothing in which you can glory, but many things for which you ought to abase yourself; for you are much weaker than you can comprehend.

3. Let nothing, then, seem much to you of all that you do.

Let nothing appear great, nothing valuable or admirable, nothing worthy of esteem, nothing high, nothing truly praiseworthy or desirable, but that which is eternal.

Let the eternal Truth please you above all things, and your own exceeding vileness ever displease you.

[1] John viii, 33, 36.

Fear nothing so much, blame and flee nothing so much, as your vices and sins, which ought to displease you more than the loss of anything whatsoever.

Some persons do not walk sincerely before Me; but led by a certain curiosity and arrogance, they desire to know My secrets and to understand the high things of God, neglecting themselves and their own salvation.

When I resist them, these often fall into great temptations and sins, because of their pride and curiosity.

4. Fear the judgements of God; dread the anger of the Almighty. Yet presume not to examine the works of the Most High; but search diligently your own iniquities, in how great things you have offended, and how much good you have neglected.

Some carry their devotions only in their books, some in pictures, and some in outward signs and figures.

Some have Me in their mouths, but there is little of Me in their hearts.

Others there are, who, enlightened in mind and purified in affection, yearn always after the things eternal. They are unwilling to hear of earthly things, and grieve to be subject to the necessities of nature. Such as these perceive what the Spirit of Truth speaks within them; for He teaches them to despise the things of the earth, and to love heavenly things; to disregard the world, and day and night to long for heaven.

CHAPTER 5

OF THE WONDERFUL EFFECT OF
DIVINE LOVE

I BLESS Thee, O heavenly Father, Father of my Lord Jesus Christ, because Thou hast vouchsafed to be mindful of me, poor as I am.

O Father of mercies, and God of all consolation,[1] I give thanks to Thee, that sometimes Thou art pleased to refresh me with Thy consolations, unworthy as I am of any consolation.

I bless Thee evermore and glorify Thee, together with Thy only-begotten Son and the Holy Ghost, the Comforter, for ever and ever.

Ah, Lord God, my holy Lover! when Thou comest into my heart, all that is within me shall exult with joy.

Thou art my glory and the exultation of my heart.

[1] 2 Corinthians i, 3.

Thou art my hope and my refuge in the day of my tribulation.[1]

2. But because I am as yet weak in love and imperfect in virtue, therefore do I need to be strengthened and comforted by Thee. Wherefore do Thou visit me often, and instruct me with Thy holy teaching.

Deliver me from evil passions, and cure my heart of all disorderly affections; so that, inwardly healed and well purified, I may become fit to love, strong to suffer, and steadfast to persevere.

3. A great thing is love, a great good every way; which alone lightens every burden and bears equally every inequality.

For it carries a burden without being burdened, and makes every bitter thing sweet and savory.

The noble love of Jesus impels a man to do great things, and ever excites him to desire that which is more perfect.

Love wills to be on high, and refuses to be held back by things below.

Love wills to be free and to be detached from all worldly affection, so that its inward vision be not hindered, and that it suffer no entanglement in temporal prosperity, or discomfiture of misfortune.

Nothing is sweeter than love, nothing stronger, nothing higher, nothing wider, nothing more pleasant, nothing fuller or better in heaven or in earth; for love is born of God, and cannot rest but in God, above all created things.

4. The lover flies, runs, and rejoices; he is free and is not bound.

He gives all for all, and has all in all; because he rests above all created things in the one Sovereign Being, from whom flows and proceeds every thing that is good.

He does not regard the gifts, but transcending all good things betakes himself to the Giver.

Love often knows no measure, but grows fervent beyond all measure.

Love feels no burden, thinks lightly of labours, aims beyond its strength, complains not of impossibility; for it conceives that all things are possible to it, and all things free.

Love, therefore, is equal to any task; and it often fulfils and succeeds, when he that does not love faints and lies prostrate.

5. Love keeps watch, and sleeping slumbers not.

Though wearied, it is not worn out; though straitened, it is not constrained; though disturbed, it is not alarmed; but, like a living flame and a burning torch, it forces its way upwards and safely passes through.

[1] Psalm lviii, 17.

If any man loves, he knows what this voice cries.

For that ardent affection of the soul is a great cry in the ears of God, and this is what it says: My God and my Love! Thou art all mine, and I am all Thine.

6. Enlarge me in love, that I may learn to taste with the inward palate of my heart how sweet it is to love, and to melt and bathe in love.

Let me be possessed by love and mount above myself from very fervour and ecstasy of love.

Let me sing love's song; let me follow Thee, my Beloved, to the heights; let my soul quite lose itself in Thy praises, rejoicing exceedingly in love.

Let me love Thee more than myself, and myself only for Thee. And in Thee let me love all who truly love Thee, as is commanded by the law of love which shines forth from Thee.

7. Love is swift, sincere, devoted, cheerful, and delightful; strong, patient, faithful, prudent, long-suffering, manly, and never self-seeking.

For when a man seeks himself, then he falls from love.

Love is circumspect, humble, upright; not soft, nor fickle, nor intent upon vain things. It is sober, chaste, steadfast, quiet, and keeps guard over all the senses.

Love is submissive and obedient to superiors; in its own eyes mean and contemptible, towards God devout and thankful; always trusting and hoping in Him, even when it does not taste the savour of God's sweetness; for there is no living in love without some sorrow.

8. Whosoever is not ready to suffer all things, and to stand resigned to the will of his Beloved, he is not worthy to be called a lover.

A lover must willingly embrace all that is hard and bitter for the sake of his Beloved, and never suffer himself to be turned away from Him by any obstacle whatsoever.

CHAPTER 6

OF THE PROOF OF A TRUE LOVER

My son, you are not yet a valiant and prudent lover.

Why so, O Lord?

Because you fall off from what you have begun upon meeting with a little adversity, and too eagerly seek after consolation.

A valiant lover stands his ground in temptations, and gives no credit to the crafty persuasions of the enemy.

As I please him in prosperity, so I do not displease him in adversity.

2. A prudent lover does not consider so much the gift of the lover as the love of the giver.

He considers the intention rather than the value, and sets the Beloved above all His gifts.

A generous lover does not rest in the gift, but in Me above every gift.

All is not therefore lost, if sometimes you have not that feeling towards Me or My Saints which you would like to have.

That good and delightful affection, which you sometimes feel, is the effect of present grace, and a sort of foretaste of your heavenly country. You ought not to lean too much upon it, because it comes and goes.

But to fight against the evil motions of the mind which come upon you, and to despise the suggestions of the devil, this is a sign of virtue and of great merit.

3. Be not troubled, therefore, if strange fancies assail you, whatsoever be their nature.

Keep your purpose firm, and your intention upright towards God.

Neither is it an illusion that sometimes you are suddenly rapt in ecstasy, and presently return to the accustomed follies of your heart.

For these you rather suffer against your will than cause them; and as long as they displease you, and you resist them, it is merit and not loss.

4. Know that the old enemy strives by all means to hinder your desire for good, and to draw you from every devout exercise: namely, from the veneration of the Saints, from the pious remembrance of My passion, from the profitable calling to mind of your sins, from watchfulness over your own heart, and from a firm purpose of advancing in virtue.

He suggests many evil thoughts, that he may cause you tedium and disgust, and so call you away from prayer and holy reading.

He is displeased with humble confession; and, if he could, he would cause you to cease from Communion.

Give no credit to him, care not for him, although he often sets his deceptive snares before your feet.

When he suggests wicked and unclean things, charge him with it and say to him:

Begone, unclean spirit! be ashamed, miserable wretch! most unclean art thou, to instil such things into my ears.

Depart from me, thou most wicked seducer; thou shalt have

no part in me; but Jesus will be with me as a valiant warrior, and thou shalt stand confounded.

I would rather die, and undergo any torment whatsoever, than consent to thee.

Hold thy peace, and be silent; I will hear thee no further, although thou many times molest me.

The Lord is my light and my salvation, whom shall I fear?[1]

If whole armies should stand together against me, my heart shall not fear.[2] *The Lord is my helper and my Redeemer.*[3]

5. Fight like a good soldier; and if sometimes you fall through frailty, take again greater courage than before, trusting in My more abundant grace. But take very great care against vain complacency and pride.

Through this many are led into error, and sometimes fall into almost incurable blindness.

They are proud and foolishly presume on themselves. Let their fall serve you as a warning and keep you always humble.

CHAPTER 7

OF CONCEALING GRACE UNDER
THE GUARDIANSHIP OF HUMILITY

MY son, it is more profitable and safer for you to hide the grace of devotion.

You should not exalt yourself, or talk greatly about it, or ponder it overmuch; but rather you should despise yourself and fear this grace, as given to one unworthy.

You must not tenaciously cleave to this state of soul, which may quickly be changed into the contrary.

When you have grace, reflect how miserable and poor you are wont to be when deprived of it.

Nor is it only when you have the grace of consolation that you make progress in the spiritual life. You make progress also when you bear the withdrawal of consolation with humility, self-denial, and patience; provided that you do not then grow remiss in the exercise of prayer, nor suffer yourself to abandon any of your accustomed good works.

According to your ability and understanding, you must do willingly what lies in your power and must not wholly neglect yourself, whatever dryness or anxiety of mind you may feel.

2. For there are many who presently grow impatient or slothful when things do not go well with them.

[1] Psalm xxvi, 1.
[2] *Ibid.*, 3.
[3] Psalm xviii, 15.

The way of man is not always in his own power. Devotion and consolation are God's gifts, and He gives them when He will, as much as He will, and to whom He will: just as it shall please Him, and no more.

Some, lacking in prudence, have ruined themselves for the sake of the grace of devotion; because they were for doing more than they could, not taking the measure of their own littleness, and following their heart's affection rather than the judgement of reason.

And as they presumptuously undertook greater things than were pleasing to God, therefore they quickly lost grace.

They that had built themselves a nest in heaven became needy and miserably abandoned, to the end that, thus humbled and impoverished, they might learn not to fly with their own wings but to have trust under Mine.

Those that as yet are but novices, and inexperienced in the way of the Lord, unless they govern themselves by the counsel of discreet men, may easily be deceived and broken.

3. And if they prefer to follow their own opinion rather than believe others who have more experience, their end will be perilous, that is, if they refuse to give up their own conceits.

Seldom do the self-wise submit to being guided by others.

It is better to have moderate knowledge and a limited intelligence, with humility, than to have great stores of learning with vain complacency.

It is better for you to be lacking in something, than to have a great deal which only makes you proud.

He does not act with sufficient discretion who gives himself up wholly to spiritual joys. He should remember his former poverty, and have that chaste fear of the Lord which dreads to lose a proffered grace.

Neither is that man wise with a truly virtuous wisdom who, when adversity or any sort of tribulation befalls him, conducts himself too despairingly, and thinks or feels about Me less trustfully than he ought.

4. He who is too secure in time of peace will often be found too much dejected and timorous in time of war.

If you could always continue humble and little in your own eyes, and keep your spirit in due order and subjection, you would not fall so easily into danger and trouble.

This is good counsel : When you have obtained the spirit of fervour, think how it will be with you when the light is withdrawn.

And when this shall happen, then remember that the light

may return again. It is as a warning to you, but for My glory, that I have withdrawn it for a time.

5. It is often more profitable for you to have such trials than that things should always go well with you and according to your will.

For a man's merits are not to be estimated by his having many visions or consolations, or by his being skilled in the Scriptures, or by his elevation to a high dignity.

But these are the tests: If he be grounded in true humility and filled with divine charity; if he seek always, purely and entirely, the honour of God; if he count himself as nothing, and sincerely despise himself; if he even be better pleased to be despised and humbled by others than honoured by them.

CHAPTER 8

OF THE MEAN ESTIMATION OF ONESELF IN THE EYES OF GOD

I WILL *speak to my Lord, though I am dust and ashes.*[1]

If I reckon myself higher than this, Thou art against me;[2] and my sins bear a true testimony which I cannot contradict.

But if I abase myself and bring myself down to very nothingness, and divest myself of all self-esteem, and account myself (as I really am) to be mere dust, then Thy grace will be favourable to me and Thy light draw nigh to my heart, and even the least self-esteem will be drowned in the depths of my own nothingness and be lost for ever.

It is there Thou showest me to myself: what I am, what I have been, and what I am come to; for I am nothing and I knew it not.

If I am left to myself, I am nothing and all weakness; but if Thou suddenly look upon me, I presently become strong, and am filled with new joy.

And truly wonderful it is that I am so quickly raised up and so graciously embraced by Thee: I who, by my own weight, am always sinking down to the lowest depths.

2. This is the work of Thy love, gratuitously forestalling and assisting me in so many necessities, preserving me also from grievous dangers, and, as I may truly say, delivering me from innumerable evils.

For, by loving myself amiss, I lost myself; and by seeking Thee alone, and purely loving Thee, I found both myself and

[1] Genesis xviii, 27.
[2] *Ibid.*, iii, 19.

Thee; and by that love have more profoundly reduced myself to nothing.

Because Thou, O most sweet Lord, dost deal with me beyond all merit of mine and beyond all that I dare hope or ask.

3. Blessed be Thou, O my God! for though I am not worthy of any benefit, yet Thy generosity and infinite goodness never cease to do good, even to those that are ungrateful and are turned far away from Thee.

Convert us to Thee, that we may be thankful, humble, and devout; for Thou art our salvation, our courage, and our strength.

CHAPTER 9

THAT ALL THINGS ARE TO BE REFERRED TO GOD AS THEIR LAST END

My son, I must be your chief and last end, if you desire to be truly blessed.

By this intention shall your affections be purified, which too often are irregularly bent upon yourself and upon creatures.

For if in anything you seek yourself, you presently faint away within yourself and grow dry.

Therefore refer all things principally to Me; for it is I that have given you all.

Consider that all things flow out from Me, who am the Sovereign Good; and therefore must they all be brought back to Me, as to their Source.

2. I am the Living Fountain, and from Me do all men draw the water of life, whether they be great men or little, whether they be rich or poor. And they that freely and willingly serve Me shall receive grace for grace.

But he that would glory in anything else besides Me, or take delight in any private good, shall not be established in true joy, nor shall he be enlarged in his heart; on the contrary, he shall in many ways be encumbered and straitened.

Therefore you ought not to ascribe any good to yourself, nor should you attribute virtue to any man; but give all to God, without whom man has nothing.

I have given all; it is My will to have all again; and with great strictness do I require a return of thanksgiving.

3. This is the truth, and by it vainglory is put to flight.

If heavenly grace and true charity enter your dwelling, there shall be in it no envy or narrowness of heart, nor shall self-love reside there.

For divine charity is all-conquering and enlarges all the powers of the soul.

If you are truly wise, you will rejoice in Me alone, you will hope in Me alone; for none is good but God only,[1] who is to be praised above all things, and in all things to be blessed.

CHAPTER 10

THAT IT IS SWEET TO DESPISE THE WORLD AND SERVE GOD

Now will I speak again, O Lord, and will not be silent; I will say in the hearing of my God, my Lord and my King, who is on high:

O how great is the abundance of Thy sweetness, O Lord, which Thou hast hidden for those that fear Thee![2]

But what art Thou to those that love Thee? what to those that serve Thee with their whole heart?

Unspeakable, indeed, is the sweetness of Thy contemplation which Thou bestowest on those that love Thee.

In this most of all hast Thou shown me the sweetness of Thy love, that when I had no being, Thou didst make me; and when I was straying far from Thee, Thou broughtest me back again that I might serve Thee; and Thou hast commanded me to love Thee.

2. O Fountain of everlasting love, what shall I say of Thee?

How can I ever forget Thee, who hast vouchsafed to remember me, even after I was corrupted and was lost?

Beyond all hope hast Thou shown mercy to Thy servant; and beyond all desert hast Thou manifested Thy grace and friendship.

What return shall I make to Thee for this favour? for it is not granted to every man to forsake all things, to renounce the world, and to take up the monastic life.

Is it much that I should serve Thee, whom the whole creation is bound to serve?

It ought not to seem much to me to serve Thee; but this rather doth appear great and wonderful to me, that Thou vouchsafest to receive for Thy servant one so wretched and unworthy, and to make him one of Thy beloved servants.

[1] Luke xviii, 19.
[2] Psalm xxx, 20.

3. Lo, all things are Thine which I have, and with which I serve Thee.

And yet contrariwise Thou rather servest me than I Thee.

Lo, heaven and earth, which Thou hast created for the service of man, stand ready before Thee, and daily perform whatsoever Thou hast commanded.

And this is but little; for Thou hast also appointed the Angels for the service of man.

But this transcends all else: that Thou Thyself hast vouchsafed to serve man, and hast promised that Thou wilt give him Thyself.

4. What shall I give Thee for all these countless favours? Would that I could serve Thee all the days of my life!

Would that I were able, were it but for one day, to serve Thee worthily!

Verily Thou art worthy of all service, of all honour, and of eternal praise.

Thou art truly my Lord, and I am Thy poor servant, who am bound with all my strength to serve Thee, and ought never to grow weary of praising Thee.

This is my will, this is my desire; and whatever is wanting in me, do Thou vouchsafe to supply.

It is a great honour, a great glory, to serve Thee, and to despise all things for Thy sake.

For they shall have great grace, who willingly subject themselves to Thy most holy service.

They shall experience the most sweet consolation of the Holy Spirit, who for the love of Thee have cast away all carnal delight.

They shall gain great freedom of mind, who for Thy name enter upon the narrow way and relinquish all worldly care.

5. O sweet and delightful service of God, which makes a man truly free and holy!

O sacred state of religious servitude, which makes men equal with the Angels, pleasing to God, terrible to the devils, and commendable to all the faithful!

O service to be embraced and ever desired, in which we merit the highest good and win that joy that shall endure for ever!

CHAPTER 11

THAT THE DESIRES OF THE HEART
ARE TO BE EXAMINED
AND CONTROLLED

My son, you have still many things to learn which you have not yet well learned.

What are these, Lord?

That in all things you conform your desire to My good pleasure: and that you be not a lover of yourself, but earnestly zealous that My will may be done.

Desires often inflame you and vehemently impel you; but consider whether you are the more moved for My honour or for your own interest.

If I am the cause, you will be well contented with whatever I shall ordain; but if there lurk in you any self-seeking, lo, this it is that hinders you and weighs you down.

2. Take care, then, not to indulge any preconceived desire without consulting Me; lest perhaps afterwards you repent, or be displeased with that which at first pleased you, and for which, as for the better thing, you were so zealous.

For not every affection which appears good is therefore at once to be followed; nor again is every contrary affection at once to be rejected.

Even in good endeavours and desires it is expedient sometimes to practise restraint; lest by too much eagerness you incur distraction of mind; lest for want of self-control you give scandal to others; or lest, by opposition from others, you suddenly become troubled and fall.

3. Sometimes, however, we must use violence and manfully resist the sensual appetite, and not regard what the flesh likes or dislikes, but rather endeavour that even though unwilling it may be subject to the spirit.

The body must be chastised and kept under servitude, until it readily obeys in all things, and learns to be content with little and pleased with simplicity, and not to murmur at any discomfort.

CHAPTER 12

OF ACQUIRING PATIENCE, AND OF
STRIVING AGAINST CONCUPISCENCE

O LORD God, I see that patience is very necessary for me, since many adversities befall us in this life.

Whatever plans I make for my peace, my life cannot be without war and pain.

That is so, My son. I would not have you seek a peace that lacks temptations or experiences no adversity; rather I would have you think you have found peace even when you are exercised by various tribulations and tried by many adversities.

2. If you say that you are not able to suffer much, how then will you endure the fire of purgatory?

Of two evils, always choose the less. And so, that you may escape eternal punishment in the future, try for God's sake to endure present evils patiently.

Do you think that men of the world suffer nothing at all or only a little? You shall not find it so, even if you seek out the most luxurious.

But you say, They have many pleasures, and they follow their own will, and therefore they make small account of their tribulations.

Granted that they have all they desire: how long do you think that this will last?

3. Lo, they that prosper in this world shall vanish like smoke,[1] and their past joys shall pass out of memory.

Nay, even whilst they live, they do not rest in the possession of them without bitterness, weariness, and fear.

From the very same things that give them delight, they often derive the punishment of sorrow.

It is just that it should be so with them. Because they seek and follow their pleasures inordinately, they should not enjoy them without trouble and bitterness.

4. O how short, how deceitful, how inordinate and shameful, are all these pleasures!

Yet, so sottish and blind are men, that they do not understand this; but, like dumb beasts, for the poor pleasures of this mortal life they incur the death of the soul.

But you, My son, *go not after your lusts, but turn away from your own will.*[2]

[1] Psalm xxxvi, 20.
[2] Ecclesiasticus xviii, 30.

Delight in the Lord, and He will give you the desires of your heart.[1]

5. Would you taste of true delight, and enjoy my consolations more abundantly? Then despise all worldly things, and cut off every base delight. So shall you receive your blessing and shall be given abundant consolation.

And the more you withdraw yourself from creaturely consolation, the sweeter and stronger consolation shall you find in Me.

But you shall not attain to this at first without some sorrow and conflict.

Ingrained habit will stand in the way but shall be overcome by better habit. The flesh will grumble but shall be curbed by fervour of spirit.

The old serpent will goad and provoke you but shall be put to flight by prayer. And, if you do but take up some useful work, the chief entry shall be closed to him.

CHAPTER 13

OF THE OBEDIENCE OF A HUMBLE SUBJECT, AFTER THE EXAMPLE OF JESUS CHRIST

MY son, he who strives to withdraw himself from obedience, withdraws himself from grace; and he that seeks private benefits, loses such as are common.

If a man does not freely and gladly submit himself to his superior, it is a sign that his flesh is not yet perfectly under control; for it often rebels and murmurs.

Therefore, if you desire to subdue your flesh, learn to obey your superior promptly.

For the outward enemy is sooner overcome, if the inward man be not laid waste.

There is not a more troublesome or worse enemy to the soul than you yourself are, when you are not in true accord with the spirit.

You must sincerely conceive a true contempt of yourself, if you wish to prevail against flesh and blood.

2. Because you still love yourself inordinately, therefore do you fear to resign yourself wholly to the will of others.

But what great matter is it, if a thing of dust and mere nothingness submits himself to man for God's sake, when I, the Almighty and the Most High, who created all things out of nothing, did for your sake humbly subject Myself to man?

[1] Psalm xxxvi, 4.

I became the most humble and most abject of all men, that you might overcome your pride by My humility.

Learn, O dust, to obey; earth and clay, learn to humble yourself, and to bow down under the feet of all.

Learn to break your own will, and to yield yourself up to all subjection.

3. Kindle wrath against yourself, suffer not the swelling of pride to live in you; but show yourself so submissive and so small that all may trample on you, and tread you under their feet as the dirt of the streets.

What have you to complain of, vain man?

What answer, wretched sinner, can you make to those that reproach you, you who have so often offended God, and so many times deserved hell?

But Mine eye has spared you, because your soul was precious in My sight; that you might know My love, and might always live thankful for My favours; that you might continually give yourself to true subjection and humility, and bear patiently the contempt that befalls you.

CHAPTER 14

OF CONSIDERING THE SECRET JUDGEMENTS OF GOD, SO THAT WE BE NOT PROUD OF ANY GOODNESS OF OURS

OVER my head, O Lord, Thou thunderest forth Thy judgements and shakest all my bones with fear and trembling; and my soul is exceedingly terrified.

I stand astonished, and consider that the heavens are not pure in Thy sight.[1]

If in the Angels Thou didst find wickedness, and didst not spare even them, what shall become of me?

Stars fell from heaven;[2] and I, dust that I am, how can I presume?

They whose works seemed praiseworthy have fallen to the very lowest depths. I have seen those that ate the bread of Angels delighted with the husks of swine.

2. There is, then, no sanctity, if Thou, O Lord, withdraw Thy hand.

No wisdom avails, if Thou cease to govern us. No strength is of any assistance, if Thou cease to preserve us. No chastity is

[1] Job xv. 14.
[2] Apocalypse viii. 10.

secure without Thy protection. No self-custody profits us, if Thy holy vigilance be not nigh to us.

For left to ourselves, we sink and perish; but visited by Thee, we are raised up and live.

We are unstable, but by Thee we are strengthened; we are lukewarm, but by Thee we are made fervent.

3. O how humbly and meanly ought I to think of myself! of how little worth ought I to esteem whatever good I seem to have!

O Lord! how profoundly ought I to abase myself under Thy unfathomable judgements, wherein I find myself to be nothing else but nothing, and altogether nothing!

O weight immense! O sea that cannot be passed over, where I discover nothing of myself save only and wholly nothing!

Where, then, is there any excuse for pride? where any room for confidence in my own virtue?

All vainglory is swallowed up in the depths of Thy judgements over me.

4. What is all flesh in Thy sight? Shall the clay glory against Him that formed it?

How can he be exalted by empty praise, whose heart is truly subjected to God?

The whole world will not exalt the man whom the Truth has subjected to itself.

Neither will the man who puts his whole hope in God be moved by the words of any that praise him.

For the speakers themselves, lo, they all are nothing, for they shall pass away with the sound of their words; but the truth of the Lord abides for ever.[1]

CHAPTER 15

HOW WE ARE TO BE DISPOSED, AND WHAT WE ARE TO SAY, WHEN WE DESIRE ANYTHING

My son, say this on every occasion: Lord, if this be pleasing to Thee, so let it be done.

Lord, if it be to Thy honour, let this be done in Thy name.

Lord, if Thou seest that this is expedient, and dost approve it as profitable for me, then grant that I may use it to Thy honour.

But, if Thou knowest that it will be hurtful to me and not profitable for the salvation of my soul, take away from me such a desire.

[1] Psalm cxvi, 2.

For not every desire is from the Holy Spirit, though to men it seem right and good.

It is difficult to judge truly whether it be a good or evil spirit that impels you to desire this or that, or whether you are not moved to it by your own spirit.

Many have been deceived in the end, who at first seemed to be led by a good spirit.

2. Whatsoever, therefore, occurs to your mind as worthy to be desired, let it be always with the fear of God and humility of heart that you desire and ask for it.

And above all you ought, with self-resignation, to commit all to Me, and to say: Lord, Thou knowest what is best; let this or that be done as Thou wilt.

Give what Thou wilt, how much Thou wilt, and at what time Thou wilt.

Do with me as Thou knowest, and as best pleaseth Thee, and is most for Thy honour.

Put me where Thou wilt, and deal freely with me in all things.

I am in Thy hand; turn me this way and that as Thou choosest.

Lo! I am Thy servant, ready for all things; for I do not desire to live for myself, but for Thee; and O that I could do so in a worthy and perfect manner!

A PRAYER THAT
THE WILL OF GOD MAY BE FULFILLED

3. Grant me Thy grace, most merciful Jesus, that it may be with me, and work with me, and continue with me to the end. Grant me always to desire and will that which is most acceptable to Thee and pleaseth Thee best.

Let Thy will be mine, and let my will always follow and agree perfectly with Thine. Let me always will, or not will, even as Thou dost; and let me not be able to will, or not to will, otherwise than as Thou dost.

4. Grant that I may die to all earthly things, and for Thy sake love to be despised and to be unknown in this world. Grant to me, above all desirable things, that I may rest in Thee and my heart find peace in Thee.

Thou art the true peace of the heart; Thou art its only rest; apart from Thee all things are devoid of comfort and rest.

In this peace, in the self-same, that is, in Thee, the one Sovereign Eternal Good, I will sleep and take my rest.[1] Amen.

[1] Psalm iv, 9.

CHAPTER 16

THAT TRUE CONSOLATION IS TO BE SOUGHT IN GOD ALONE

WHATSOEVER I can desire or imagine for my comfort, I do not look for it here but hereafter.

For if I alone should have all the comforts of this world, and might enjoy all its delights, certain it is that they could not last long.

Wherefore, O my soul, you cannot be fully comforted or perfectly refreshed except in God, the Comforter of the poor and the Supporter of the humble.

Wait a little while, my soul, wait for the divine promise, and you shall have abundance of all good things in heaven.

If you desire these present things inordinately, you shall lose those that are heavenly and eternal.

Use temporal things, but desire eternal.

You cannot be satisfied with any temporal goods, because you were not created for the enjoyment of such things.

2. Although you had all created goods, you could not be happy and blessed; but in God, who created all things, consist all your beatitude and happiness.

And that happiness is not such as is seen or cried up by the foolish lovers of the world, but such as the good faithful of Christ look for, and of which the spiritual and clean of heart, whose conversation is in heaven, have sometimes a foretaste.

Vain and brief is all human comfort.

Blessed and true is that comfort which is derived inwardly from the Truth.

A devout man everywhere carries about with him Jesus his Consoler, and he says to Him: Be with me, O Lord Jesus, in all places and at all times.

Let this be my consolation, to be glad to forgo all human comfort.

And if Thy consolation be withdrawn, let Thy will and Thy just trial be to me as the greatest of consolations.

For Thou wilt not always be angry, nor wilt Thou threaten for ever.[1]

[1] Psalm cii, 9.

CHAPTER 17

THAT ALL OUR CARES
ARE TO BE CAST UPON GOD

MY son, let Me do with you what I will; I know what is expedient for you.

You think as a man; you judge in many things as human affection suggests.

Lord, what Thou sayest is true. Greater is Thy care for me than all the care I can take of myself.

For he stands very precariously, who casts not his whole care on Thee.

Lord, provided that my will remain true and firm towards Thee, do with me whatsoever shall please Thee.

For it cannot but be good, whatever Thou shalt do with me.

2. If Thou wilt have me to be in darkness, be Thou blessed; and if Thou wilt have me to be in light, be Thou again blessed; if Thou vouchsafe to comfort me, be Thou blessed; and if it be Thy will that I should be afflicted, be Thou still equally blessed.

My son, thus must you stand affected, if you desire to walk with Me : You must be as ready to suffer as to rejoice; you must be as glad to be poor and needy as to be full and rich.

3. Lord, I will suffer willingly for Thee whatsoever Thou art pleased should befall me.

I am willing indifferently to receive from Thy hand good and evil, sweet and bitter, joy and sorrow; and to give Thee thanks for all that happens to me.

Keep me from all sin, and I will fear neither death nor hell.

Provided that Thou dost not cast me off for ever, nor blot me out of the book of life:[1] no matter what tribulation befalls me, it shall not hurt me.

[1] Apocalypse iii, 5.

CHAPTER 18

THAT TEMPORAL MISERIES ARE TO BE BORNE WITH EQUANIMITY, AFTER THE EXAMPLE OF CHRIST

MY son, I came down from heaven for your salvation; I took upon Me your miseries, moved not by necessity but by charity; that you might learn patience, and bear without repining the miseries of this life.

For from the hour of My birth until My death upon the cross, I was not without suffering.

I suffered great want of all earthly things; I frequently heard many complaints against Me; I endured calmly disgrace and reproaches; for benefits I received ingratitude; for miracles, blasphemies; for teaching, reproofs.

2. O Lord, because Thou wast patient in Thy lifetime, herein especially fulfilling the commandment of Thy Father, it is fitting and according to Thy will that I, a wretched sinner, should bear myself patiently, and for my salvation carry the burden of this corruptible life as long as Thou shalt please.

For, although this present life be burdensome, yet by Thy grace it has been rendered very meritorious; and by Thy example and the footsteps of Thy Saints, more tolerable and glorious for the weak.

Also, it is much more full of consolation than it was formerly under the old Law, when the gate of heaven remained shut; and even the way thither seemed darksome, when so few cared to seek the Kingdom of Heaven.

Moreover, they who were then just and meet to be saved, could not enter into Thy heavenly Kingdom before Thy passion and the atonement of Thy sacred death.

3. O what great thanks am I bound to render Thee, for having vouchsafed to show me and all the faithful the right and good way to Thine everlasting Kingdom!

For Thy life is our way; and by holy patience we walk unto Thee, who art our Crown.

If Thou hadst not gone before us and instructed us, who would care to follow?

Alas, how many would stay a great way behind, had they not before their eyes Thy glorious example!

We are still lukewarm, though we have heard of so many miracles and teachings of Thine! What then would happen, had we not so great a light whereby to follow Thee?

CHAPTER 19

OF BEARING INJURIES, AND WHAT MAN IS
PROVED TRULY PATIENT

WHAT is it you say, My son? Cease your complaining, and consider My passion, and the sufferings also of the Saints.

You have not yet resisted unto blood.

Little is it that you suffer, in comparison of those who suffered so much; who were so strongly tempted, so grievously afflicted, so many ways tried and exercised.

You ought then to call to mind the heavier sufferings of others, that you may the more easily bear the very little things you suffer.

And if to you they do not seem very little, take heed lest this also proceeds from your impatience.

But whether they be little or great, strive to bear them all with patience.

2. The better you dispose yourself for suffering, the more wisely do you act, and the more do you merit; and you will bear it more easily if both in mind and by habit you are diligently prepared for it.

Do not say: I cannot endure these things from such a man, and things of this kind are not to be suffered by me; for he has done me a great injury, and he upbraids me with things I never thought of; but from another I will willingly suffer these things, and will regard them as things I ought to suffer.

Such a thought is foolish; for it considers not the virtue of patience, nor by whom it shall be crowned, but weighs rather the persons, and the wrongs done to oneself.

3. He is not a truly patient man who will suffer no more than he thinks good, and only from whom he pleases.

The truly patient man minds not by what manner of man it is that he is exercised, whether by his own superior, whether by an equal, or by an inferior; whether by a good and holy man, or by one that is perverse and unworthy.

But how much soever and how often soever any adversity happens to him from any creature, he takes it all equally with thanksgiving as from the hand of God, and esteems it a great gain.

For nothing that is suffered for His sake, however trifling it be, shall go unrewarded by God.

4. Therefore, be prepared to fight, if you desire to gain

the victory. Without conflict you cannot attain the crown of patience.

If you will not suffer, you refuse to be crowned; if you desire to be crowned, fight manfully, and endure patiently.

Without labour there is no coming to rest, nor without fighting do we reach victory.

O Lord, make that possible to me by grace, which seems impossible to me by nature. Thou knowest I can bear but little, and that I am soon dejected when a small adversity arises.

Let all exercises of tribulation become lovely and desirable to me for Thy Name's sake; for to suffer and to be afflicted for Thee is very wholesome for my soul.

CHAPTER 20

OF THE CONFESSION OF OUR OWN WEAKNESS, AND OF THE MISERIES OF THIS LIFE

I WILL *confess against myself my injustice;*[1] I will confess to Thee my weakness, O Lord.

It is often a small thing that casts me down and troubles me.

I purpose to behave myself valiantly; but when even a small temptation comes, I am brought into great straits.

Sometimes it is a mere trifle that gives rise to a serious temptation.

I am thinking myself safe enough and have no apprehension of danger, when suddenly I find myself almost overcome as by a mere breath of wind.

2. Therefore, O Lord, regard my wretchedness and frailty, which are completely known to Thee.

Have pity on me and draw me out of the mire, so that I may not stick fast therein and be utterly cast down for ever.

What often dismays and confounds me in Thy sight is this, that I am so feeble and frail in resisting my passions.

And even though I do not go so far as to consent to them, yet their assaults are troublesome and grievous to me, and I am very weary of living in this daily state of conflict.

My weakness is made known to me especially by this, that abominable imaginations invade my mind far more readily than they depart.

3. Most mighty God of Israel, zealous lover of faithful

[1] Psalm xxxi, 5.

souls! O that Thou wouldst regard the labour and sorrow of Thy servant, and stand by him in all his undertakings!

Strengthen me with heavenly fortitude, lest the old man, the miserable flesh not fully subdued to the spirit, prevail and get the upper hand; against which we must fight so long as we breathe in this most wretched life.

Alas, what a life is this, where afflictions and miseries are never wanting, where all round us are snares and enemies!

For when one tribulation or temptation is gone, another comes; yes, even while the first conflict still lasts, many others come on, and those unexpected.

4. And how is it possible that the life of man can be loved, which has so great bitternesses, and is subject to so many calamities and miseries?

How even can it be called life, which begets so many deaths and plagues?

And yet it is loved, and many seek their delight in it.

The world is often censured as deceitful and vain; and yet it is with reluctance abandoned, because the desires of the flesh bear so great a sway.

Some things draw us to love the world; others to despise it.

The lust of the flesh, the lust of the eyes, and the pride of life:[1] these draw us to the love of the world; but the pains and miseries, which justly follow, breed a hatred and loathing of it.

5. Yet it is true, more's the pity, that vicious pleasure dominates the mind of the worldling and he thinks it delightful to shelter amid thorns,[2] because he has neither seen nor tasted the sweetness of God and the inward charm of virtue.

But such as perfectly despise the world and endeavour to live for God under holy discipline, these men are not unacquainted with the divine sweetness that is promised to true renunciation. And they see clearly how gravely the world is mistaken and in many ways deceived.

CHAPTER 21

THAT WE ARE TO REST IN GOD ABOVE ALL GOODS AND GIFTS

ABOVE all things, and in all things, my soul, rest always in the Lord, for He is the eternal rest of the Saints.

Grant me, O most sweet and loving Jesus, to repose in Thee above all things created, above all health and beauty, above

[1] 1 John ii, 16.
[2] Job xxx, 7.

all glory and honour, above all power and dignity, above all knowledge and subtlety, above all riches and arts, above all joy and gladness, above all fame and praise, above all sweetness and consolation, above all hope and promise, above all merit and desire, above all gifts and presents that Thou canst give and infuse, above all joy and jubilation that the mind can receive and feel: in fine, above Angels and Archangels and all the host of heaven, above all things visible and invisible, and above all that is not Thee, my God.

2. For Thou, O Lord my God, art supremely good above all things; Thou alone art most high, Thou alone most powerful, Thou alone most full and most sufficient, Thou alone most sweet and most full of consolation.

Thou alone art most beautiful and most loving, Thou alone most noble and most glorious above all things; in whom all good things together both perfectly are, and ever have been, and ever shall be.

And therefore all is too little and insufficient whatever Thou bestowest upon me besides Thyself, or whatever Thou revealest to me concerning Thyself, or promisest, so long as I do not see Thee, nor fully possess Thee. For surely my heart cannot truly rest nor be entirely contented, unless it rest in Thee,[1] and transcend every gift and every creature.

3. O Thou most beloved Bridegroom of my soul, Christ Jesus, Thou most pure Lover, Thou Lord of the whole creation! who will give me the wings of true liberty, that I may fly away and rest in Thee?

O when shall it be granted me to be free from all else, and to see how sweet Thou art, O Lord my God?

When shall I fully gather up myself in Thee, that for love of Thee I may not feel my self, but Thee alone, above all sense and measure, in a manner not known to all?

But now I often lament, and bear with grief my unhappiness.

Because many evils happen in this vale of miseries, which frequently disturb me, sadden me, and cast a cloud over me. Often do they hinder and distract me, allure and entangle me, so that I can neither have free access to Thee, nor enjoy Thy sweet embraces, which are ever open to the blessed spirits.

4. O Jesus, brightness of eternal glory, comfort of the pilgrim soul! let my sighs move Thee, and my manifold desolation here on earth.

In Thy presence my mouth is dumb, and my silence it is that speaks to Thee.

How long does my Lord delay to come? Let Him come to me, His poor servant, and make me joyful. Let Him stretch

[1] St Augustine, *Confessions* 1, i.

forth His hand, and deliver me in my misery from all anguish.

Come, O come! for without Thee no day nor hour shall be joyful; for Thou art my joy, and without Thee my table is empty.

I am wretched and like one imprisoned and loaded with fetters, till Thou refresh me with the light of Thy presence, and set me free, and show a friendly countenance towards me.

5. Let others seek what they please instead of Thee; nothing else pleases or shall please me but Thou, my God, my hope and my eternal salvation.

I will not hold my peace, nor cease to pray, until Thy grace return, and Thou speakest inwardly to me in this way:

Lo, here I am; lo, I come to you, because you have called upon Me. Your tears and the desire of your soul, your humiliation and contrition of heart, have inclined and brought Me to you.

And I said: O Lord, I have called upon Thee, and have desired to enjoy Thee, being ready to spurn all things for Thy sake.

For Thou didst first move me that I should seek Thee.

Blessed be Thou therefore, O Lord, who hast shown this goodness to Thy servant, according to the multitude of Thy mercies.

6. What more has Thy servant to say in Thy presence? save that he humble himself exceedingly before Thee, mindful always of his own iniquity and vileness.

For there is none like unto Thee amongst all the wonders of heaven and earth.

Thy works are exceedingly good, Thy judgements true, and by Thy providence are all things governed.

Praise therefore and glory be to Thee, O Wisdom of the Father; let my tongue, my soul, and all things created, join in praising Thee and blessing Thee.

CHAPTER 22

OF THE REMEMBRANCE OF GOD'S MANIFOLD BENEFITS

O LORD, open my heart in Thy law, and teach me to walk in Thy commandments.

Give me to understand Thy will, and to remember with great reverence and diligent consideration all Thy benefits, as well in general as in particular, that so henceforward I may be able worthily to give Thee thanks for them.

I know and confess indeed, that I am not able to return Thee due thanks of praise, not even for the least. I am less than any of Thy benefits bestowed upon me; and when I consider Thy excellence, my spirit faints before its greatness.

2. All things that we have in soul and body, and whatsoever we possess outwardly or inwardly, naturally or supernaturally, all are Thy benefits, and do proclaim Thee bountiful, loving and good; from Thee we have received all blessings.

Although one has received more, another less, yet all these blessings are Thine, and without Thee even the least cannot be had.

He who has received greater blessings cannot glory because of his own merit, or exalt himself above others, or scorn him who has less. For that man is truly greater and better, who attributes less to himself, and is more humble and devout in returning thanks.

And he who esteems himself the vilest of all men, and judges himself the most unworthy, is best fitted to receive still greater blessings.

3. But he who has received fewer ought not to be saddened, or take it ill, or envy him that is richer. He should attend rather to Thee, and very much praise Thy goodness, because Thou bestowest Thy gifts so plentifully, so freely and willingly, without respect of persons.

All things are from Thee, and therefore Thou art to be praised in all.

Thou knowest what is expedient to be given to each. Why this one has less, and the other more, is not for us to decide but for Thee, by whom are determined the merits of each.

4. Wherefore, O Lord God, I even deem it a great benefit not to have much which outwardly and in the eyes of men might appear praiseworthy and glorious. For a man ought to be so far from conceiving trouble, or sadness, or dejection at his own poverty and lowliness, that on the contrary he takes consolation from them and great joy.

For Thou, O God, hast chosen the poor and the humble, and those that are despised by this world,[1] for Thy familiar friends and members of Thy household.

Thy Apostles themselves are witnesses, whom Thou hast made princes over the whole earth.[2]

And yet they lived in this world without complaint, so humble and simple, so free from malice or guile, that they even rejoiced to suffer reproaches for Thy name,[3] and embraced with great affection the things which the world shrinks from.

[1] 1 Corinthians i, 27, 28.
[2] Psalm xliv, 17.
[3] Acts v, 41.

5. Nothing, therefore, ought to give so great joy to one that loves Thee and knows Thy benefits as the accomplishment of Thy will in himself, and the good pleasure of Thy eternal decrees.

With which he ought to be so far contented and consoled, that he would just as willingly be the least as another would wish to be the greatest; and would enjoy as much peace and content in the lowest place as in the highest; and would be as willing to be despised and an outcast, of no name and repute, as to be honoured above the rest of men and greater in the world than they.

For Thy will and the love of Thy honour ought to take precedence of all things; they should console and please him better than all the benefits which he has had or shall yet have.

CHAPTER 23

OF FOUR THINGS THAT BRING MUCH PEACE

My Son, I will now teach you the way of peace and of true liberty.

Do, Lord, as Thou sayest, for I shall be glad to hear the lesson.

Study, My son, to do the will of another rather than your own.

Choose always to have less rather than more.

Seek always the lowest place, and to be subject to every one.

Desire always and pray that the will of God may be entirely fulfilled in you.

Lo, such a one enters within the borders of peace and rest.

2. O Lord, this short lesson of Thine contains in itself much perfection.

It is short in words, but full of meaning and rich in fruit.

If I could but faithfully observe it, I should not be so easily troubled.

For as often as I find myself disquieted and disturbed, I discover that I have strayed from this doctrine.

But Thou, O Lord, who canst do all things, and always lovest the profit of the soul, give me yet greater grace, that I may be able to fulfil Thy lesson and accomplish my salvation.

A PRAYER AGAINST EVIL THOUGHTS

3. *O Lord my God, depart not far from me; make haste to*

help me:[1] for there have risen up against me various thoughts and great fears, afflicting my soul. How shall I pass through them without hurt? how shall I break them in pieces?

Thus says the Lord: *I will go before you and will humble the great ones of the earth.* I will open the gates of the prison, and will reveal to you hidden secrets.[2]

Do, Lord, as Thou sayest, and let all wicked thoughts fly from before Thy face.

This is my hope and my sole comfort, to fly to Thee in all tribulations, to confide in Thee, to call on Thee from my inmost heart, and patiently to wait for Thy consolation.

A PRAYER FOR THE ENLIGHTENING OF THE MIND

4. Enlighten me, O good Jesus, with the brightness of inward light, and cast out all darkness from the dwelling of my heart.

Restrain my many wandering thoughts, and destroy the temptations that violently assault me.

Fight strongly for me, and overcome the evil beasts, that is to say, the alluring desires of the flesh; that so there may be peace in Thy power,[3] and the abundance of Thy praise may resound in Thy holy court, that is, in a clean conscience.

Command the winds and the storms. Say to the sea: Be still, and to the north wind: Blow thou not; and there shall be a great calm.[4]

5. Send forth Thy light and Thy truth,[5] that they may shine upon the earth; for I am an earth that is empty and void,[6] till Thou enlightenest me.

Pour forth Thy grace from above; drop upon my heart the dew of heaven; supply fresh streams of devotion, to water the face of the earth, that it may bring forth good and perfect fruit.

Lift up my mind, oppressed with the load of sins, and raise my whole desire towards heavenly things; that having tasted the sweetness of supernal happiness, I may dislike to think of the things of earth.

6. Tear me away, and rescue me from all unstable comfort of creatures; for no created thing can fully appease and comfort my desire.

[1] Psalm lxx, 12.
[2] Isaias xlv, 2, 3.
[3] Psalm cxxi, 7.
[4] Matthew viii, 26.
[5] Psalm xlii, 3.
[6] Genesis i, 2.

Join me to Thyself with an inseparable bond of love; for Thou alone art sufficient for the soul that loveth Thee, and without Thee all things are vain and worthless.

CHAPTER 24

OF AVOIDING CURIOUS INQUIRY INTO ANOTHER'S LIFE

MY son, be not curious, and do not pursue idle cares.

What is this or that to you? Follow Me.

For what is it to you whether that man be such or such, or whether this man do or speak this or that?

You do not need to answer for others; it is for yourself that you shall give an account. Why, therefore, do you meddle with them?

Lo, I know all men, and do see all things that are done under the sun; and I know how it is with every one, what he thinks, what he would have, and at what his intention aims.

To Me, therefore, are all things to be committed; but do you keep yourself in perfect peace, and let the unquiet be as unquiet as he will.

Whatsoever he does or says, he shall be punished for it, for he cannot deceive Me.

2. Be not solicitous for the shadow of a great name,[1] nor for acquaintance with many, nor for the particular love of individuals.

For these things beget distractions and great darkness in the heart.

I would gladly speak My word to you and reveal My secrets, if you would diligently observe My coming, and open to Me the door of your heart.

Be circumspect, watch in prayer, and humble yourself in all things.

[1] St Bernard, from Lucan i, 135.

CHAPTER 25

WHEREIN CONSIST FIRM PEACE OF THE HEART AND TRUE PROGRESS

MY son, I have said: *Peace I leave to you, My peace I give to you; not as the world gives, do I give to you.*[1]

Peace is what all desire; but all do not care for those things which belong to true peace.

My peace is with the humble and meek of heart; in much patience shall your peace be.

If you will hear Me, and follow My voice, you may enjoy much peace.

What, then, shall I do, Lord?

In everything attend to yourself, what you are doing and what you are saying; and direct your whole intention to this, that you may please Me alone; and neither desire nor seek anything besides Me.

And as for the sayings or doings of others, judge nothing rashly, neither busy yourself with things not committed to your care; and thus may it be brought about that you shall be little or seldom disturbed.

2. But never to feel any disturbance at all, nor suffer any trouble of heart or body: this is not the condition of our present life, but of everlasting rest.

Think not, therefore, that you have found true peace, if you feel no trouble; nor that then all is well, if you have no adversary; nor that you have attained to perfection, if all things be done according to your desire.

Neither do you then conceive a great notion of yourself, or imagine yourself to be especially beloved, if you experience great devotion and sweetness; for it is not in such things as these that a true lover of virtue is known; nor do the progress and perfection of a man consist in these things.

3. In what, then, O Lord?

In offering yourself with your whole heart to the Divine Will; not seeking your own interests either in little or great, either in time or in eternity.

So shall you with the same serenity continue to give thanks both in prosperity and adversity, weighing all things in an equal balance.

If you come to be so valiant and long-suffering in hope,

[1] John xiv. 27.

that when inward consolation is withdrawn you can prepare your heart to suffer still more; and if you do not justify yourself, as if you ought not to suffer such and so great things, but acknowledge Me to be just in all My appointments, and praise My holy Name: then it is that you walk in the true and right way of peace, and may entertain an undoubting hope to see My face again with great joy.

And, if you arrive at an entire contempt of yourself, know that then you shall enjoy an abundance of peace, as much as is possible in this your earthly sojourn.

CHAPTER 26

OF THE EXCELLENCE OF A FREE MIND WHICH IS TO BE GOT BY HUMBLE PRAYER RATHER THAN BY STUDY

LORD, this is the work of a perfect man: never to let the mind slacken from attending to heavenly things, and amidst many cares to pass on as it were without care; not after the manner of a dullard, but by a certain privilege of a free mind, cleaving to no creature with inordinate affection.

2. Preserve me, I beseech Thee, O most gracious Lord God, from the cares of this life, that I be not too much entangled by them; from the many necessities of the body, that I be not ensnared by pleasure; and from all hindrances of the soul, lest I be broken by trouble and quite overthrown.

I do not ask to be preserved from those things which worldly vanity covets with so much eagerness; but from those miseries which by the common curse of our mortality do penally depress the soul of Thy servant and keep him back from entering as often as he would into liberty of spirit.

3. O my God, who art unspeakable sweetness, turn for me into bitterness all carnal consolation which withdraws me from the love of things eternal, and wickedly allures me to itself, by setting before me some delightful present good.

Let me not be overcome, O my God, let me not be overcome by flesh and blood; let not the world and its transitory glory deceive me; let not the devil and his cunning trip me up.

Give me courage to resist, patience to endure, and constancy to persevere.

Give me, instead of all worldly consolation, the most sweet unction of Thy Spirit; and instead of carnal love, infuse into me the love of Thy name.

4. Lo! food, drink, clothing, and other necessaries for the

maintenance of the body, all are burdensome to the fervent spirit.

Grant that I may use my necessary sustenance with moderation, and not be entangled with any inordinate appetite.

It is not lawful to cast it all away, for nature must be sustained; but to require superfluities, and such things as are rather for delight, Thy holy law forbids; for then the flesh would rebel against the spirit.

In all this, I beseech Thee, let Thy hand govern and teach me, that there may be no excess.

CHAPTER 27

THAT IT IS SELF-LOVE CHIEFLY WHICH DELAYS US FROM REACHING THE SOVEREIGN GOOD

My son, you must give all for all and be nothing of your own.

Know that the love of yourself is more hurtful to you than anything in the world.

In proportion to the love and affection which you have for them, so do things cleave to you.

If your love be pure, simple, and well-ordered, you shall not be in captivity to anything.

Covet not that which you may not have.

Seek not to have that which may embarrass you and deprive you of your inward liberty.

It is wonderful that you will not, from the very bottom of your heart, commit yourself wholly to Me, with all things that you can have or desire.

2. Why do you pine away with vain grief? why are you so worn with superfluous cares?

Abide by My good pleasure and you shall suffer no loss.

If you seek this or that, or would be here or there for your own convenience and the more to indulge your own will, you will never be at rest, nor free from solicitude; for in everything there will be found some defect, and in every place there will be some one that will cross you.

3. Your welfare, therefore, does not lie in obtaining and multiplying external things, but rather in contemning them and utterly rooting them out of your heart. And this I would have you understand not only of money and riches, but also of the ambition of honour and the desire of empty praise: all which things pass away with the world.

The place avails little, if the spirit of fervour be lacking. Nor shall that peace last long which is sought from without, if there be no true foundation in the heart. This means that, unless you rely upon Me, you may change yourself, but you shall not make yourself better.

For, when opportunity occurs and is seized, you shall find that which you fled from, and more still.

A PRAYER FOR THE CLEANSING OF THE HEART AND FOR HEAVENLY WISDOM

4. Confirm me, O God, by the grace of Thy Holy Spirit. Grant me power to be strengthened in the inner man, and to empty my heart of all useless cares and anxieties. Let me not be drawn away by sundry desires of anything whatsoever, be it worthless or precious, but let me look on all things as passing away, and myself also as passing with them.

For nothing is lasting under the sun, but all is vanity and vexation of spirit.[1] O how wise is he who thus judges!

5. Grant me, O Lord, heavenly wisdom, that I may learn above all things to seek Thee and find Thee, above all things to relish Thee and love Thee, and to understand all other things as they are, according to the order of Thy wisdom.

Grant that I may prudently avoid him that flatters me, and patiently bear with him that contradicts me.

For this is great wisdom, not to be moved with every wind of words, nor to give ear to the wicked, flattering siren; for thus shall we go on securely in the way we have begun.

CHAPTER 28

AGAINST THE TONGUES OF SLANDERERS

MY son, take it not to heart if some people think ill of you, and if they say of you what you do not like to hear.

You ought to think worse things of yourself, and to believe that there is no one weaker than yourself.

If you walk inwardly, you will make small account of fleeting words.

It is no small prudence to keep silence in the evil time, to turn inwards to Me, and not to be disturbed by the judgements of men.

2. Let not your peace depend on the tongues of men. For whether they put a good or a bad construction on what you do, you are still what you are.

---

[1] Ecclesiastes i, 14.

Where are true peace and true glory? Are they not in Me?

And he that neither desires to please men, nor fears to displease them, shall enjoy much peace.

From inordinate love and vain fear arise all disquiet of heart and distraction of mind.

CHAPTER 29

THAT WE MUST CALL UPON GOD AND BLESS HIM, WHEN TRIBULATION PRESSES

BLESSED be Thy name for ever, O Lord, who hast been pleased that this trial and tribulation should come upon me.

I cannot escape it, but must needs fly to Thee, that Thou mayest help me and turn it to my good.

Lord, I am now in tribulation, and my heart is ill at ease; for I am much afflicted with my present suffering.

And now, Beloved Father, what shall I say? I am taken, Lord, in these straits; O save me from this hour.[1]

Yet for this reason have I come to this hour,[2] that Thou mayest be glorified, when I am greatly humbled and then by Thee delivered.

May it please Thee, O Lord, to deliver me;[3] for, poor wretch that I am! what can I do, and whither shall I go without Thee?

Give me patience, O Lord, even now at this hour.

Help me, O my God, and I shall not be afraid, how much soever I may be distressed.

2. And now, in the midst of these things, what shall I say? Lord, Thy will be done.[4] I have well deserved to be afflicted and distressed.

Surely I ought to bear it; and O that I may bear it with patience, until the tempest pass over and a better time come.

Yet Thy almighty hand is able to take away from me this temptation also, and to moderate its violence, that I sink not altogether under it. Even so hast Thou often done before, O my God, my Mercy!

And the more difficult it is for me, so much the easier to Thee is this change of the right hand of the Most High.[5]

[1] John xii, 27.
[2] *Loc. cit.*
[3] Psalm xxxix, 14.
[4] Matthew vi, 10.
[5] Psalm lxxvi, 11.

CHAPTER 30

OF ASKING GOD'S HELP, AND OF TRUST
IN THE RECOVERY OF GRACE

MY son, I am the Lord who gives strength in the day of tribulation.[1] Come to Me, when it is not well with you.

This it is which most of all hinders heavenly consolation, that you are too slow in betaking yourself to prayer.

For before you earnestly pray to Me, you seek in the meantime many comforts, and refresh yourself in outward things.

And hence it comes that all things avail you little, till you consider well that I am He who delivers those that trust in Me; nor is there out of Me any powerful help, or profitable counsel, or lasting remedy.

But now, regaining breath after the storm, grow strong again in the light of My mercies; for I am at hand, says the Lord, to repair all, not only to the full, but even with abundance and above measure.

2. Is anything difficult to Me? Or shall I be like to one promising and not performing?

Where is your faith? Stand firmly and perseveringly; practise endurance and manly courage; consolation will come to you in due season.

Wait for Me, wait; I will come and cure you.

It is a temptation that vexes you, and a vain fear that affrights you.

What does solicitude about future contingencies bring you, but only sorrow upon sorrow? *Sufficient for the day is the evil thereof.*[2]

It is vain and useless to have either grief or joy for future things, which perhaps shall never come to pass.

3. But it is in human nature to be deluded with such imaginations; and it is the sign of a soul as yet weak, to be so easily drawn away by the suggestions of the enemy.

For he cares not whether he deludes and deceives you with things true or false; whether he overthrows you with the love of things present, or the fear of things to come.

So, let not your heart be troubled, nor let it be afraid.[3]

Believe in Me, and trust in My mercy.

[1] Nahum i, 7.
[2] Matthew vi, 34.
[3] John xiv, 27.

When you think you are far from Me, I am often nearer to you.

When you judge that almost all is lost, then are you often on the road to greater merit.

All is not lost when anything falls out contrary to your wishes.

You must not judge according to your present feeling. Whencesoever trouble comes, you must not so give in to it or take it so, as if all hope of deliverance were gone.

4. Think not yourself wholly forsaken, though for a time I have sent you some tribulation, or even withdrawn from you your wished-for consolation; for this is the way to the Kingdom of Heaven.

And without doubt it is more expedient for you and for the rest of My servants that you be exercised in adversity, than that you should have all things according to your desires.

I know your secret thoughts, and that it is very expedient for your salvation that you sometimes be left without any savour of sweetness, lest perchance you be conceited about your success, and be well-pleased with yourself, imagining that you are what you are not.

What I have given, I have the power to take away, and to restore as it pleases Me.

5. When I have given it, it is still Mine; when I withdraw it, I do not take anything of yours; for every best gift and every perfect gift is Mine.[1]

If I send you any affliction or adversity, repine not; neither let your heart be cast down.

I can quickly raise you up again, and turn every burden into joy.

Nevertheless, I am just and greatly to be praised when I thus deal with you.

If you think aright and consider things truly, you ought never to be so much dejected and troubled at adversity.

But you should rather rejoice and give thanks, and even account it a special subject of joy, that I afflict you with sorrows and do not spare you.

As the Father has loved Me, I also love you,[2] said I to My beloved disciples; whom certainly I did not send to temporal joys, but to great conflicts; not to honours, but to contempt; not to idleness, but to labours; not to rest, but to bring forth much fruit in patience. Remember these words, O My son.

[1] James i, 17.
[2] John xv, 9.

CHAPTER 31

OF DESPISING ALL CREATED THINGS, THAT SO WE MAY FIND THE CREATOR

O LORD, I stand in much need of yet greater grace, if I am to get so far that no man and no created thing can hinder me.

For so long as anything holds me back, I cannot fly freely to Thee.

He was desirous of flying freely to Thee who said: *Who will give me the wings of a dove, and I will fly and be at rest?*[1]

What is more at rest than the eye that is single?

And what is more free than he that desires nothing on earth?

Therefore a man ought to transcend everything created, to forsake himself perfectly, and to stand in ecstasy of mind and see that Thou, the Creator of all, hast nothing like to Thee among creatures.

Unless a man be detached from all created things, he cannot attend freely to things divine.

And this is the reason why there are found so few contemplative persons, because there are few that know how to sequester themselves entirely from perishable creatures.

2. For this a great grace is required, such as may elevate the soul, raising her up above herself.

And unless a man be elevated in spirit, freed from attachment to all creatures, and wholly united to God, whatever he knows, and whatever he has, is of no great importance.

Long shall he be little, and lie grovelling below, who esteems anything great but only the one, immense, eternal Good.

Whatsoever is not God is nothing, and ought to be accounted as nothing.

There is a great difference between the wisdom of an enlightened and devout man and the knowledge of a learned and studious clerk.

Far more noble is that learning which flows from above, by divine infusion, than that which is laboriously acquired by the wit of man.

3. Many are found to desire contemplation, but they are not careful to practise those things which are required for its attainment.

It is a great hindrance that we rest in signs and sensible things, and have but little perfect mortification.

I know not what is the matter, by what spirit we are led,

[1] Psalm liv, 7.

or what we pretend to, we who seem to be called spiritual persons. We take infinite pains and are full of solicitude about transitory and worthless things, and we seldom or never think with full recollection of the things of our soul.

4. Alas, after a slight recollection, we presently break forth again; neither do we weigh our deeds well, by a strict examination.

We mind not where our affections lie. We do not deplore the impurity that is in all our actions.

The great Deluge came because all flesh had corrupted its way.[1]

So, when our inward affections are much corrupted, it must needs be that the action which follows should also be corrupt, proceeding as it does from a weakened heart. But, if the heart be pure, it yields the fruit of a good life.[2]

5. We ask how much a man has done; but we do not consider so studiously how great was the virtue with which he acted.

We ask whether he be strong, rich, handsome, clever, a good writer, a good singer, or a good workman; but how poor he is in spirit, how patient and meek, how devout and inward: these are things of which few men speak.

Nature considers the outward man, but grace turns to the inward.

Nature is often in error; but grace puts her trust in God and therefore is not deceived.

CHAPTER 32

OF SELF-DENIAL AND THE RENUNCIATION OF ALL CUPIDITY

MY son, you cannot possess perfect liberty, unless you deny yourself wholly.

All self-seekers and self-lovers are bound in fetters. They are full of desires, full of cares, ever unsettled; and always they seek their own comfort, not the things of Jesus Christ. They busy themselves often in fashioning and framing something which cannot last. For everything shall perish that does not come from God.

Hold fast this short and perfect word: Forsake all, and you shall find all; relinquish base desire, and you shall find rest.

[1] Genesis vi, 12.
[2] Matthew vii, 16.

Consider this well; and when you have put it into practice, you shall understand all things.

2. Lord, this is not the work of one day, nor is it child's play; nay, in this short sentence is comprised all the perfection of the religious life.

My son, you ought not to be deterred or at once dejected, when you hear of the way of perfection; rather should you be drawn on to those higher things, or at least aspire ardently to their attainment.

I would it were so with you, and that you had come so far, that you were no longer a lover of yourself, but did simply wait upon my bidding and upon the bidding of the father whom I have set over you. Then would you greatly please Me, and all your life would pass in joy and peace.

You have yet many things to forsake. Unless you give them up to Me without reserve, you shall not obtain that for which you ask.

I counsel you, so that you may become rich, to buy of Me gold tried in the fire,[1] that is, the heavenly wisdom which tramples under foot all earthly things.

Lay aside earthly wisdom, that is, all human respect and self-complacency.

3. I mean that you must buy for yourself things which are considered worthless, and in exchange give what men think precious and noble.

For very cheap, and of little account, and well-nigh forgotten by men, seems that true and heavenly wisdom, which teaches no high notions of self, nor seeks to be magnified upon earth. Many praise it in their words, while in their life they are far from it. Yet this same wisdom is the pearl of great price,[2] which is hidden from many.

CHAPTER 33

OF INCONSTANCY OF HEART, AND OF DIRECTING
OUR FINAL INTENTION TO GOD

MY son, trust not to your feeling; whatever it may be now, it will quickly be changed into something else.

As long as you live, you are subject to change, whether you will or no. At one time you are merry, at another sad; now at peace, and now troubled; now devout, and now indevout; now fervent, and now sluggish; now grave, and now gay.

[1] Apocalypse iii, 18.
[2] Matthew xiii, 46.

But he that is wise and well instructed in spirit, stands above all these changes, not minding what he feels in himself, nor in what quarter the wind of instability blows, but seeking only this: that the whole intent of his soul shall work towards the due and desired end.

2. For thus can he continue one and the same and unperturbed, and contrive amid all the variety of events to direct the single eye of his intention unceasingly towards Me.

And the purer the eye of his intention is, with so much the greater constancy does he pass through various storms.

But in many the eye of pure intention grows dim; for they quickly look towards something delightful that comes in their way; and seldom will you find any one altogether free from all blemish of self-seeking.

So of old the Jews came to Bethany, to Martha and Mary, *not for Jesus' sake only, but also that they might see Lazarus.*[1]

The eye of the intention must therefore be cleansed that it may be single and right; and it must be directed to Me, beyond all those manifold things that come between.

CHAPTER 34

THAT GOD IS SWEET ABOVE ALL THINGS AND IN ALL THINGS, TO THE SOUL THAT LOVES HIM

THOU art my God and my all![2] What would I have more, and what greater happiness can I desire?

O sweet and delicious word! but to him only that loves the Word, not the world nor the things that are in the world.

My God and my all! To the man that understands, enough is said; and to repeat it often is delightful to him that loves.

For when Thou art present, all things yield delight; but when Thou art absent, all things grow loathsome. Thou makest a tranquil heart, and great peace, and festal joy.

Thou makest us to think well of all things, and in all things to praise Thee; nor can anything without Thee afford any lasting pleasure; but if it is to be agreeable and well-pleasing to us, it must be accompanied by Thy grace and be seasoned with the savour of Thy wisdom.

2. To him that finds savour in Thee, what will not taste aright? But what can ever bring joy, to him that savours Thee not?

The worldly-wise, and those that savour the things of the

[1] John xii, 9.
[2] 1 Corinthians xv, 28.

flesh, are deficient in true wisdom; for in the world is found much vanity, and in the flesh is death.

But they that follow Thee, despising the world and mortifying the flesh, are seen to be truly wise; for they are translated from vanity to truth, and from the flesh to the spirit.

Such as these find savour in God; and, whatever good is found in creatures, they refer it all to the praise of their Maker.

But great, yes, very great, is the difference between the savour of the Creator and of the creature, of eternity and of time, of the light uncreated and of created light.

3. O Light perpetual, transcending all created light! flash forth Thy lightning from above, that it may penetrate all the secret recesses of my heart.

Cleanse, cheer, enlighten, and enliven my spirit with all its powers, that with joyful ecstasy it may cleave to Thee.

O when will that blessed and desirable hour come, that Thou mayest fill me with Thy presence, and become to me all in all?

So long as this is not granted me, my joy will not be full.

As yet, alas, the old man is living in me; he is not wholly crucified; he is not perfectly dead.

He still lusts strongly against the spirit and wages war within me; neither does he suffer the kingdom of the soul to be at peace.

4. But Thou, that rulest the power of the sea and stillest the motion of its waves,[1] arise and help me.

Scatter Thou the nations that delight in war;[2] crush them in Thy might.

Show forth, I beseech Thee, Thy wonderful works, and let Thy right hand be glorified.

For there is no other hope or refuge for me save in Thee, O Lord my God.

CHAPTER 35

THAT THERE IS NO BEING SECURE FROM TEMPTATION IN THIS LIFE

My son, you are never secure in this life; as long as you live you have need always of spiritual armour.

You dwell in the midst of enemies and are assaulted on the right hand and on the left.

[1] Psalm lxxxviii, 10.
[2] Psalm lxvii, 31.

Unless therefore you defend yourself on every side with the shield of patience, you will not be long without a wound.

Moreover, unless you set your heart fixedly on Me, with a sincere will of suffering all things for My sake, you shall not be able to bear the stress of this warfare, nor to win the crown of the Blessed.

Therefore must you go through all manfully, and use a strong hand against whatsoever opposes you.

For to him that overcomes is given manna,[1] but to the sluggard is left much misery.

2. If you seek rest in this life, how then will you come to rest everlasting?

Set not yourself for much rest, but for great patience.

Seek true peace, not upon earth, but in heaven; not in men nor in other creatures, but in God alone.

You must for the love of God suffer all things gladly: labour and sorrow, temptation, vexation, anxiety, necessity, infirmity, injury, detraction, reproof, humiliation, shame, correction and contempt.

These things help to virtue; they prove the novice of Christ; they weave a celestial crown.

In return for this brief labour I will give you an eternal reward, and for transitory shame, everlasting glory.

3. Do you think to have spiritual consolations always, whenever you please?

My Saints had not so; they met with many troubles, and various temptations, and great desolations.

But they bore all with patience and trusted more in God than in themselves, knowing that *the sufferings of this time are not worthy to be compared with the glory to come,*[2] which is our goal.

Would you have that immediately, which others have hardly obtained after many tears and great labours?

Wait upon the Lord, do manfully, and be of good heart,[3] do not despond, do not fall away, but with constancy offer both soul and body for the glory of God.

I will reward you most abundantly; I will be with you in all your tribulations.[4]

[1] Apocalypse ii, 17.
[2] Romans viii, 18.
[3] Psalm xxvi, 14.
[4] Psalm xc, 15.

CHAPTER 36

AGAINST THE VAIN JUDGEMENTS OF MEN

MY son, cast your heart firmly upon the Lord. Fear not the judgement of men, when your conscience testifies that you are good and guiltless.

It is a good and blessed thing to suffer in such manner; neither will this be grievous to a humble man that trusts in God rather than in himself.

Many men say many things, and therefore little credit must be given to them. Neither is it possible to satisfy all.

Though Paul endeavoured to please all in the Lord, and became all things to all men,[1] yet he made little account of being judged by man.[2]

2. He laboured abundantly for the edification and salvation of others, with all his might and main; but he could not escape being judged and despised by others.

Therefore he committed all to God who knew all, and defended himself by patience and humility against the tongues of those that spoke unjustly, as well as against those who devised vain and lying deceits and threw out their slanders at random.

However, he answered them sometimes, lest his silence might give occasion of scandal to the weak.

3. Who are you that you should be afraid of a mortal man?[3] To-day he is, and to-morrow he is no more to be seen.

Fear God, and you shall not be afraid of the terrors of men.

What can any one do against you by words or affronts?

He hurts himself rather than you; nor shall he be able, whoever he be, to escape the judgement of God.

Have God before your eyes, and do not contend in querulous words.

And though for the present you seem to be worsted, and to suffer a shame which you have not deserved, do not repine at this, and do not lessen your crown by impatience. But rather look up to Me in heaven, who am able to deliver you from all shame and wrong, and to render to every one according to his works.[4]

[1] 1 Corinthians ix, 22.
[2] *Ibid.*, iv, 3.
[3] Isaias li, 12.
[4] Matthew xvi, 27.

CHAPTER 37

OF A PURE AND ENTIRE RESIGNATION OF OUR-
SELVES FOR THE OBTAINING FREEDOM
OF HEART

My son, forsake yourself, and you shall find Me.

Stand without choice or any self-seeking, and you shall always gain.

For greater grace shall at once be added to you when you give up yourself, and do not take yourself back again.

Lord, how often shall I resign myself, and in what things shall I forsake myself?

Always and at all times; as in little things, so also in great. I make no exception, but will have you to be found in all things stripped naked.

Otherwise, how can you belong to Me and I to you, unless you be both inwardly and outwardly stripped of your own will?

The sooner you effect this, the better will it be with you; and the more fully and sincerely you do it, the more will you please Me, and the more shall you gain.

2. Some there are that resign themselves, but it is with certain exceptions; for they do not wholly trust in God, and therefore are they busy in providing for themselves.

Some also at first offer all; but afterwards, being assailed by temptation, they return again to their own ways and therefore make no progress in virtue.

These shall neither attain to the true liberty of a pure heart, nor to the grace of a delightful familiarity with Me, unless they first entirely resign themselves, and offer themselves a daily sacrifice to Me. Without this, the union of fruition neither does nor shall subsist.

3. I have very often said to you, and I repeat it now again: Forsake yourself, resign yourself, and you shall enjoy a great inward peace.

Give all for all; seek nothing; call for nothing back; stand purely and with a full confidence before Me, and you shall possess Me.

You shall be free in heart, and the darkness shall not cover you.[1]

Strive for this, pray for this, long for this: that you may be stripped of all self-seeking, and thus naked follow Jesus naked; that you may die to yourself and live eternally to Me.

[1] Psalm cxxxviii, 11.

Then shall every vain fancy cease, and all evil disturbance of mind, and all needless care.

Then also immoderate fear shall depart, and inordinate love shall die.

CHAPTER 38

OF THE GOOD GOVERNMENT OF OURSELVES IN OUTWARD THINGS, AND OF HAVING RECOURSE TO GOD IN DANGERS

MY son, you ought diligently to aim at this, that in every place, and in every action or outward occupation, you be inwardly free and master of yourself; that all things be under you, and not you under them; and that you be lord and ruler of your actions, and not a slave or a hireling.

Rather you should be a freeman and a true Hebrew,[1] transferred to the lot and the liberty of the sons of God.[2]

They stand above things present, and contemplate the eternal; with the left eye they regard transitory things, and with the right those of heaven.

Temporal things draw them not away to cleave to them; but they rather draw these things so that they may subserve aright the end for which they were ordained by God and appointed by that Sovereign Artist, who has left nothing disordered in His whole creation.

2. Moreover, if in all events you depend not upon things as they appear outwardly, nor regard with a carnal eye things seen and heard, but on every occasion enter like Moses into the tabernacle to consult the Lord, you shall sometimes hear the divine answer, and shall return instructed about many things present and future.

For Moses always had recourse to the tabernacle for the deciding doubts and questions, and fled to the aid of prayer for succour against the dangers and wickedness of men.

So must you, in like manner, fly to the closet of your heart, and there most earnestly implore the divine assistance.

For we read, that for this cause were Joshua and the children of Israel deceived by the Gabaonites, because they did not first consult the Lord;[3] but too easily giving credit to fair words, they were deluded by counterfeit piety.

[1] John i, 47.
[2] Colossians i, 12; Romans viii, 21.
[3] Joshua ix, 14.

CHAPTER 39

THAT A MAN MUST NOT BE OVER-EAGER IN HIS AFFAIRS

MY son, always commit your cause to Me; I will dispose of it well in its due season.

Await My disposal, and you shall find it for your advantage.

Lord, most willingly do I commit all things to Thee; for my own cogitations can little avail.

Would that I did not so much dwell upon future events, but unhesitatingly offered myself to Thy good pleasure.

2. My son, a man often vehemently pursues something which he desires; but when he has attained it, he begins to be of another mind.

For our affections are not wont to continue long upon the same object, but rather drive us from one thing to another.

It is therefore important for a man to forsake himself, even in the most trifling things.

3. Man's true progress consists in denying himself; and the man of self-denial is very free and very secure.

But the old enemy, opposed to all that are good, ceases not from tempting, but day and night lies in ambush, hoping to entrap the unwary in his deceitful snares.

The Lord says: *Watch and pray, that ye enter not into temptation.*[1]

CHAPTER 40

THAT MAN HAS NO GOOD OF HIMSELF AND CANNOT GLORY IN ANYTHING

LORD, *what is man, that Thou art mindful of him; or the son of man, that Thou visitest him?* [2]

What has man deserved, that Thou shouldst give him Thy grace?

Lord, what cause have I to complain, if Thou forsake me? or what can I justly allege, if Thou dost not grant what I ask.

This most assuredly I may truly think and say: Lord, I am nothing, I can do nothing, I have nothing of myself that is good; but in all things do I fail, and do ever tend to nothing.

[1] Matthew xxvi, 41.
[2] Psalm viii, 5.

And unless I am assisted and inwardly instructed by thee, I become wholly lukewarm and slack.

2. But Thou, O Lord, art always the self-same,[1] and endurest to eternity; ever good, just, and holy; doing all things well, justly, and holily; and disposing them in wisdom.

But I, who am more inclined to go back than to go forward, do not continue ever in the same state; for seven times are passed over me.[2]

Yet it soon becomes better with me when it pleases Thee and Thou stretchest out Thy helping hand; for Thou alone, without man's aid, canst so assist and strengthen me that my countenance shall no more be changed,[3] but my heart be converted and find its rest in Thee alone.

3. Wherefore, did I but know well how to cast from me all human consolation, either for the sake of gaining devotion, or through the necessity which compels me to seek Thee, since no man can comfort me: then might I deservedly hope in Thy favour, and rejoice in the gift of new consolation.

4. Thanks be to Thee, from whom all proceeds, whenever things go well with me.

I, indeed, am in Thy sight but vanity and nothingness, an inconstant and feeble man.

In what therefore can I glory, or for what do I desire to be held in esteem?

Is it for my very nothingness? That too is most vain.

Truly vain-glory is an evil plague, the greatest of vanities; because it draws us away from true glory, and robs us of heavenly grace.

For whilst a man takes complacency in himself, he displeases Thee; while he seeks human applause, he is deprived of true virtue.

5. This is true glory and holy exultation: to glory in Thee, and not in oneself; to rejoice in Thy name, and not in one's own virtue; to find pleasure in no creature, save only for Thy sake.

Let Thy Name be praised, not mine; let Thy work be magnified, not mine; let Thy Holy Name be blessed; but let me take to myself none of the praises that men utter.

Thou art my glory, Thou art the joy of my heart.

In Thee will I glory and rejoice all the day; but for myself I will glory in nothing but in my infirmities.[4]

6. Let the Jews seek that glory which one man gives to another; I will seek that glory which is from God alone.

---

[1] Psalm ci, 28.
[2] Daniel iv, 22.
[3] 1 Kings i, 18.
[4] 2 Corinthians xii, 5.

All human glory, all temporal honour, all worldly dignity, compared to Thy eternal glory, are but vanity and folly.

O my God, my Truth and my Mercy! O Blessed Trinity! to Thee alone be praise, honour, power, and glory, world without end.

CHAPTER 41

OF THE CONTEMPT OF ALL TEMPORAL HONOUR

MY son, take it not to heart if you see others honoured and exalted, and yourself despised and degraded.

Lift up your heart to Me in heaven, and the contempt of men on earth shall not grieve you.

Lord, we are blind and are quickly seduced by vanity. If I look well into myself, there never was any undeserved injury done me by any creature, and therefore I can have no just complaint against Thee.

2. I have often and grievously sinned against Thee, and therefore every creature justly takes up arms against me.

Therefore, confusion and contempt are my due; but Thou art entitled to praise and honour and glory.

And unless I dispose myself to be willing and glad to be despised and forsaken by all creatures, and to be esteemed altogether nothing, I cannot gain inward peace and stability, nor be spiritually enlightened and fully united to Thee.

CHAPTER 42

THAT PEACE IS NOT TO BE PLACED IN MEN

MY son, if you place your peace in any person, moved by your feelings and by desire of his company, you shall be unsettled and entangled.

But, if you have recourse to the ever-living and abiding Truth, you shall not be greatly grieved if a friend forsake you or die.

Your love for a friend ought to be grounded in Me; for Me ought he to be loved, whosoever in this life seems to you good and very dear.

Without Me friendship has no worth or endurance; nor is that love true and pure which is not based upon Me.

You ought to be so dead to such friendly affections, that you would choose for your part to be without any human fellowship.

Man draws the nearer to God, the further he withdraws himself from all earthly solace.

So much the higher also does he ascend to God, the lower he descends in himself, and the viler he becomes in his own estimation.

2. But he that attributes anything of good to himself, hinders God's grace from coming into him; for the grace of the Holy Spirit ever seeks a humble heart.

If you could treat yourself as mere nothingness and empty your heart of all created love, then must I pour out great grace upon you.

When you look towards creatures, the countenance of the Creator is withdrawn from you.

Learn, for the sake of the Creator, to overcome yourself in all things; and then shall you be able to attain divine knowledge.

If anything, however little, be inordinately loved and regarded, it keeps you back from God and corrupts the soul.

CHAPTER 43

AGAINST VAIN AND WORLDLY LEARNING

My son, let not the fair and subtle sayings of men affect you; for the Kingdom of God is not in speech but in power.[1]

Attend to My words, for they enkindle hearts and enlighten minds, excite to compunction and afford manifold consolation.

Never read anything in order that you may appear more learned or more wise.

Strive to overcome evil habits, for this will profit you more than the knowledge of many difficult questions.

2. When you have read much and know many things, you must always return to the one Beginning.

I am He who teaches men knowledge;[2] and I give little children a clearer understanding than can be taught by man.

He to whom I speak, shall quickly be wise, and shall make great progress in spirit.

Woe to them that inquire about many curious things, and care little about the way to serve Me.

The time will come, when Christ, the Master of masters,

---

[1] 1 Corinthians iv, 20.
[2] Psalm xciii, 10.

the Lord of Angels, shall appear to hear the lessons of all men, that is, to examine every conscience.

And then will He search Jerusalem with lamps,[1] and the hidden things of darkness shall be brought to light, and the arguments of tongues shall be silent.

I am He that in an instant raises the humble mind to understand more principles of eternal Truth than can be learnt by ten years in the schools.

I teach without noise of words, without confusion of opinions, without ambition of honour, without strife of arguments.

I am He who teaches men to despise earthly things, to loathe things present, to seek and to relish the things eternal, to fly honours, to endure scandals, to place all hope in Me, to desire nothing out of Me, and above all things ardently to love Me.

3. There was a man who, by loving Me intimately, learned things divine and spoke wonders. He profited more by forsaking all things than by studying subtleties.

But to some I speak things common, to others things more particular; to some I sweetly appear in signs and figures, whilst to others in a great light I reveal mysteries.

A book has but one voice; yet it does not instruct all men alike. For within the soul am I, the Teacher, the Truth, the Searcher of the heart, the Understander of thoughts, the Mover of actions: giving unto every man as I shall judge meet.

CHAPTER 44

OF NOT DRAWING TO OURSELVES OUTWARD THINGS

My son, in many things you must be ignorant, and esteem yourself as one dead upon the earth, and as one to whom the whole world is crucified.

You must also pass by many things with a deaf ear, and think rather on the things that are for your peace.

It is more profitable to turn away your eyes from such things as displease you, and to leave to every man his own way of thinking, than to indulge in contentious disputes.

If you stand well with God and regard His judgement, you will more easily bear to be overcome.

2. O Lord, to what a pass are we come? A temporal loss is bewailed; for a small gain men labour and run; but spiritual loss is overlooked and hardly ever remembered.

[1] Sophonias i, 12.

That which is of little or no profit takes up our thoughts, and that which is necessary above all is negligently passed over. For the whole man runs away after outward things; and unless he quickly come to himself, he is content to wallow in those outward things.

CHAPTER 45

THAT WE MAY NOT BELIEVE ALL MEN; AND HOW EASILY WE ERR IN SPEECH

GRANT *me help, O Lord, in my tribulation, for vain is the salvation of man.*[1]

How often have I found faithfulness lacking where I thought I could count on it.

How often too have I found it where I least expected it!

Vain therefore is hope in men; in Thee, O God, is the salvation of the just.

Blessed be Thou, O Lord my God, in all things that befall us.

We are weak and unstable; we quickly fail and quickly change.

2. Who is the man that can keep himself so warily and so circumspectly in all things, as not sometimes to fall into delusion or perplexity?

But he that trusts in Thee, O Lord, and seeks Thee with a simple heart, does not so easily fall.

And if he fall into some tribulation and be greatly involved in it, yet shall he quickly be rescued or comforted by Thee; for Thou wilt not forsake him that trusts utterly in Thee.

3. Rare indeed is the faithful friend that remains constant throughout all the trials of his friend.

Thou, O Lord, Thou alone art most faithful in all things; and there is none other like to Thee.

O how wise was that holy soul that said: *My mind is firmly established and grounded in Christ.*[2]

Were it so with me, human fear would not so easily give me anxiety, nor the arrows of men's words move me.

4. Who is able to foresee all things? Who can provide against future evils?

If things foreseen do yet often hurt us, how can unexpected things do otherwise than grievously wound us? But why did I not provide better for my wretched self? Why too have I so easily placed my confidence in others?

[1] Psalm lix, 13.
[2] St Agatha. The Breviary, February 5th.

But we are men, and nothing else but frail men, although by many we are esteemed and called angels.

To whom shall I give credit, O Lord? To whom but to Thee? Thou art the Truth, which can neither deceive nor be deceived.

And on the other hand, every man is a liar,[1] weak, unstable, and fallible, especially in words. And therefore we ought not readily to believe everything that seems to sound well.

5. How wisely didst Thou forewarn us to *beware of men,* and that *a man's enemies are those of his own household,* and that we *are not to believe if any one should say: Lo here, or lo there.*[2]

I have been taught this lesson to my cost; and I wish it may serve to make me more cautious, and not to increase my folly.

A man says to me: Take care, take great care, keep what I tell you to yourself.

And so I do, and believe the matter to be secret; yet he himself cannot keep the secret which he desired me to keep, but presently betrays both me and himself, and goes his way.

From such foolish speech and such silly people defend me, O Lord, that I may not fall into their hands, nor ever commit the like.

Give truth and constancy to the words of my mouth, and remove a crafty tongue far from me.

I ought to take great care not to do to others what I hate to have done to myself.

6. O how good it is, and what peace it brings, to be silent about others, not believing all that is said, nor readily repeating it; to confide in few men, while always seeking Thee, the Beholder of the heart; not to be carried about this way and that by every wind of words; and in all things, whether of soul or body, to desire the accomplishment of the good pleasure of Thy will!

How safe it is, for the preservation of heavenly grace, to shun all human display, not seeking those things that appear to win public admiration, but rather pursuing with our whole diligence the things that bring amendment of life and fervour!

7. How much harm has been suffered by men because their virtue became known and was then too hastily commended! And, on the other hand, what profit has accrued when grace has been protected by silence! Such is the condition of this frail life of ours, which is truly accounted nothing but trial and conflict.[3]

---

[1] Romans iii, 4.
[2] Matthew x, 17, 36; xxiv, 23.
[3] Job vii, 1.

CHAPTER 46

OF HAVING CONFIDENCE IN GOD WHEN THE ARROWS OF WORDS ASSAIL US

My son, stand firm, and trust in Me; for what are words but words?

They fly through the air, but cannot do any real hurt.

If you are guilty, resolve willingly to amend; if you are conscious of no fault, be ready to suffer this for God's sake.

It is not much that you should sometimes suffer words, who are not yet able to endure hard blows.

And why do such trifles affect you, except because you are still carnal and regard men more than you ought?

Because you are afraid of being despised, you are unwilling to be blamed for your faults, and seek shelter in excuses.

2. But look better into yourself, and you shall find worldliness still in your heart and a vain desire to please men.

You refuse to be abased and put to shame for your faults, so that it is plain that you are not truly humble or dead to the world, nor is the world crucified to you.

But give ear to My word, and you shall not mind ten thousand words of men.

If all things were said against you which the utmost malice could possibly invent, what hurt could they do you, if you would let them all pass and value them no more than a straw?

Could they so much as pluck even one hair from your head?

3. But the man who does not enter into himself, nor keep God before his eyes, is easily moved with a word of blame. Whereas he that trusts in Me, and has no desire to stand by his own judgement, shall be free from the fear of men.

For I am the Judge and Discerner of all secrets; I know well how the matter passed; I know who inflicted the injury and who suffered it.

From Me went forth this word; by My permission has this thing happened, that the thoughts of many hearts may be made manifest.[1]

I shall be the Judge of the guilty and the innocent; but I have willed to try them both beforehand with a secret judgement.

4. The testimony of men often deceives, but My judgement is true; it shall stand and shall not be overthrown.

For the most part it is hidden, and fully manifest to few; yet

[1] Luke ii, 35.

it never errs, nor can it err, though to the eyes of the unwise it may not seem right.

To Me, therefore, should you run in every judgement, and not rely upon your own opinion.

For the just man shall not be disturbed, whatsoever shall befall him from God.

And even should some unjust charge be preferred against him, he will not greatly care. Yet neither will he vainly rejoice, if through the intervention of others he be justly acquitted.

5. For he considers that I am He who searches the heart and the reins;[1] who judges not according to outward show and the notions of men.

For often that is found blameworthy in My eyes which in the judgement of men is thought praiseworthy.

O Lord God, the just Judge, strong and patient,[2] who knowest the frailty and depravity of men: be Thou my strength and my whole confidence, for my own conscience does not suffice for me.

Thou knowest that which I know not; and therefore under every rebuke I ought to humble myself and suffer meekly.

Pardon me, therefore, in Thy mercy, for not having acted so in the past; and give me in future the grace of greater endurance.

Thy abundant mercy is better for me, for the obtaining of pardon, than any self-righteous defence of my secret conscience.

And although I am not conscious to myself of anything, yet I cannot hereby justify myself; for, except through Thy mercy, no living man shall be justified in Thy sight.[8]

CHAPTER 47

THAT ALL GRIEVOUS THINGS ARE TO BE ENDURED FOR THE SAKE OF LIFE EVERLASTING

My son, be not crushed by the labours which you have undertaken for My sake nor let tribulations ever depress you; but in every occurrence be strengthened and consoled by My promise.

I am well able to reward you, beyond all measure and degree.

You shall not labour here long, nor shall you always be oppressed with sorrows.

[1] Apocalypse ii, 23 (Psalm vii, 10).
[2] Psalm vii, 12.
[8] Psalm cxlii, 2.

Wait a little while, and you shall see a speedy end of suffering.

There shall come an hour when all labour and trouble will cease. Little and brief is all that passes with time.

2. Whatever you do, do it with a will. Labour faithfully in My vineyard; I will be your reward.

Write, read, sing, lament, keep silence, pray, bear adversities manfully: eternal life is worth all those battles, and greater than those.

Peace shall come on a day which is known to the Lord.

And there shall be no day nor night like those of this present time; but light everlasting, infinite brightness, steadfast peace, and safe repose.

You shall not then say: *Who shall deliver me from the body of this death?* [1] Neither shall you cry out: *Woe is me, that my sojourning is prolonged!* [2] For death shall be cast down headlong, and there shall be never-ending life, with no anguish any more, but blessed joy and fellowship sweet and lovely.

3. O if you were to see the everlasting crowns of the Saints and what great glory they now enjoy who formerly appeared contemptible to the world and even unworthy of life! Doubtless you would immediately cast yourself down to the ground, and would desire rather to be in subjection to all men than to have precedence over so much as one.

Neither would you covet the pleasures of this life, but would be glad rather to suffer tribulation for God's sake, and would esteem it the greatest gain to be reputed worthless by men.

4. O if you did but appreciate these things and take them deeply to heart, would you venture to complain even once?

Are not all labours to be endured for the sake of everlasting life? This is the great question: Shall I win or lose the Kingdom of God?

Therefore, lift up your eyes to heaven. Lo, there am I, and with Me all My Saints, who in this world fought a great fight. They now rejoice, are now comforted, are now secure, are now at rest. And so they shall abide with me in the Kingdom of My Father for all eternity.

[1] Romans vii, 24.
[2] Psalm cxix, 5.

CHAPTER 48

OF THE DAY OF ETERNITY, AND OF THE TRIALS OF THIS LIFE

O MOST blessed mansion of the celestial city! O most bright day of eternity, never darkened by any night, but ever irradiated by the Sovereign Truth!

O day always joyful, always secure, and never changing to darkness!

O that that day had dawned, and that all these temporal things had come to an end!

For the Saints, indeed, that day shines, resplendent with everlasting brightness; but we pilgrims upon earth see it only from afar, and as through a glass.[1]

2. The citizens of heaven know how joyful is that day; but we, poor banished children of Eve,[2] mourn this our own day as bitter and tedious.

The days of this life are few and evil,[3] full of griefs and trials. Here man is defiled by many sins, ensnared by many passions, enslaved by many fears, harassed by many cares, distracted by many curiosities, entangled by many vanities, encompassed by many errors, worn out by many labours, troubled by temptations, enervated by pleasures, tormented by want.

3. O when shall there be an end to these evils? When shall I be set at liberty from the wretched slavery of sin? When, O Lord, shall I think of Thee alone? When shall I fully rejoice in Thee?

When shall I enjoy true liberty without any hindrance, without any affliction of soul or body?

When shall there be solid peace, peace secure and undisturbed, peace within and without, peace every way assured?

O good Jesus! when shall I behold Thee? When shall I contemplate the glory of Thy Kingdom? When wilt Thou be all in all to me?

O when shall I be with Thee in Thy Kingdom, which Thou hast prepared for Thy beloved ones from all eternity?

I am left, poor and an exile, in an enemy's country, where there are daily wars and grievous misfortunes.

4. Console me in my banishment, soothe my sorrow, for my

[1] 1 Corinthians xiii, 12.
[2] From the *Salve Regina*.
[3] Genesis xlvii, 9.

whole desire aspires to Thee. For whatever this world offers for my comfort, all this is burdensome to me.

I long to enjoy Thee most inwardly, but I cannot attain to this joy.

I desire to cleave to heavenly things, but I am weighed down by things temporal and by my unmortified passions.

With my mind I wish to be above all things, but in the flesh I am forced against my will to be subject to them.

Thus, unhappy man that I am,[1] I fight with myself and am burdensome to myself, whilst the spirit tends upwards and the flesh downwards.

5. O how much I suffer inwardly, when I am meditating upon heavenly things and presently a crowd of carnal thoughts interrupts me as I pray.

O my God, be not far from me, nor turn away in wrath from Thy servant.[2]

Flash forth Thy lightning, and scatter them; shoot out Thine arrows,[3] and let all the phantoms of the enemy be routed.

Cause my senses to be recollected in Thee; make me forget all wordly things; grant me speedily to cast away and despise all sinful imaginations.

Come to my aid, O eternal Truth, that no vanity may move me.

Come, heavenly Sweetness, and let all impurity flee from before Thy face.

Pardon me also, and mercifully forgive me, as often as in my prayer I think of anything else besides Thee.

For I truly confess that I am wont to have very many distractions.

For many a time I am not there where I am bodily standing or sitting, but am there rather where my thoughts carry me. There am I where my thought is: and there often is my thought where is the thing that I love.

That thing most readily comes to my mind which naturally delights me or through custom is pleasing to me.

6. Whence Thou, the Truth, hast plainly said: *Where thy treasure is, there is thy heart also.*[4]

If I love heaven, I willingly think on heavenly things.

If I love the world, I rejoice in worldly prosperity and am troubled in the time of adversity.

If I love the flesh, my imagination is often on the things of the flesh.

If I love the spirit, I delight to think of spiritual things.

---

[1] Romans vii, 24.
[2] Psalm lxx, 12.
[3] Psalm cxliii, 6.
[4] Matthew vi, 21.

For whatever things I love, of the same I willingly speak and hear, and I carry home with me the images of such things.

But blessed is that man who for Thee, O Lord, bids farewell to all things created; who offers violence to nature, and through fervour of spirit crucifies the lusts of the flesh. Such a one, with a serene conscience, shall offer Thee pure prayer. And, having shut out all earthly things, both outwardly and inwardly, he shall become worthy to be admitted to the angelic choirs.

CHAPTER 49

OF THE DESIRE OF ETERNAL LIFE, AND HOW
GREAT REWARDS ARE PROMISED TO THOSE
THAT STRIVE

MY son, when you perceive that the desire of eternal bliss is being infused into you from above, so that you would fain go out of the tabernacle of this body in order to contemplate My glory that suffers no shadow of change:[1] enlarge your heart and welcome this holy visitation with your whole desire.

Return the greatest thanks to the Supernal Goodness, which deals so condescendingly with you, mercifully visits you, ardently incites you, and powerfully supports you, lest by your own weight you fall down to the things of earth.

For it is not by your own thought or endeavour that you receive this visitation, but by the mere condescension of heavenly grace and divine regard; that so you may advance in virtue and greater humility, prepare yourself for future conflicts, labour with the whole affection of your heart to keep close to Me, and serve Me with a fervent will.

2. My son, the fire often burns, but the flame does not ascend without smoke. Even so, the desires of some are on fire after heavenly things, and yet they are not free from the temptation of carnal affection.

Therefore it is not altogether for God's honour alone that they act, when they put their earnest petitions before Him.

Of the same nature frequently is your own desire, which you have represented as so earnest.

For that desire is not pure and perfect which is alloyed with self-interest.

3. Ask not for what is pleasant and convenient to you, but rather for what is acceptable to Me and for My honour. For,

[1] James i, 17.

if you judge rightly, you ought to prefer and to follow My appointment rather than your own desire or any desirable thing.

I know your desire, and I have heard your many groanings.

You would wish already to be enjoying the liberty of the glory of the children of God.

Already your delight is set upon your eternal home, the heavenly fatherland, where is fulness of joy.

But the time for that is not yet come; for there is still another time, namely, a time of war, a time of labour and trial.

You desire to be filled with the Sovereign Good, but you cannot attain that now.

I am who am, says the Lord; wait for Me, until the Kingdom of God shall come.[1]

4. As yet must you be tried upon earth and exercised in many things.

Consolation shall sometimes be given you, but its abundant fulness is not granted.

Take courage, therefore, and be valiant,[2] as well in doing as in suffering those things that go counter to nature.

You must put on the new man and be changed into another person.

That which you would not, you must often do; and that which you would, you must leave undone.

What pleases others shall prosper; what is pleasing to you shall not succeed.

What others say shall be hearkened to; what you say shall be reckoned as nought.

Others shall ask, and shall receive; you shall ask, and shall not obtain.

5. Others shall be great in the mouths of men; about you none shall speak.

To others this or that shall be committed; but you shall be accounted as fit for nothing.

At this nature will sometimes repine; and it will be a great matter if you bear it in silence.

In these, and many such-like things, the faithful servant of the Lord is wont to be tried, to see how far he can deny himself and in all things break down self.

There is scarcely anything in which you so much need to die to yourself as in seeing and suffering things that go counter to your will; and this more especially when something is commanded that seems to you unsuitable and of little use.

And because, being under authority, you dare not resist

[1] Luke xxii, 18.
[2] Joshua i, 7.

the higher power, therefore it seems to you hard to walk at the beck of another and wholly to give up your own opinion.

6. But consider, My son, the fruit of these labours, their speedy termination, and their reward exceeding great; and you will not derive affliction but the strongest comfort from your patience.

For in return for that little will which you now freely forsake, you shall for ever have your will in heaven.

For there you shall find all that you will, and all that you can desire.

There shall you have the possession of every good, without fear of losing it.

There your will shall always be one with Mine, and shall not covet any extraneous or private thing.

There no one shall resist you, no one complain of you, no one obstruct you, nothing stand in your way; but every desirable good shall be present at the same moment, shall refresh all your affections and satiate them to the full.

There I will give you glory for the contumely you have suffered; a garment of praise in return for sorrow;[1] and instead of the lowest place, a royal throne for ever.

There shall the fruit of obedience appear, there shall the labour of penance rejoice, and humble subjection shall be gloriously crowned.

7. Now, therefore, bow yourself down humbly under the hands of all, and heed not who it was that said or commanded this thing or that.

But let it be your great care, that whether your superior, or inferior, or equal, require anything of you, or suggest anything, you take all in good part, and labour with a sincere will to perform it.

Let one man seek this, another that; let this man glory in this thing, another in that; and let him be praised a thousand thousand times. For your part, however, rejoice neither in this nor in that, but in the contempt of yourself and in My good pleasure and honour alone.

Let this be your wish: Whether by life or by death, may God always be glorified in me.[2]

---

[1] Isaias lxi, 3.
[2] Philippians i, 20; 1 Peter iv, 11.

CHAPTER 50

THAT A DESOLATE MAN OUGHT TO OFFER HIMSELF INTO THE HANDS OF GOD

O LORD God, holy Father, be Thou now and for ever blessed; for as Thou wilt, so is it done, and what Thou dost is always good.

Let Thy servant rejoice in Thee, not in himself nor in any other; for Thou alone art true joy, Thou art my hope and my crown, Thou art my joy and my honour, O Lord.

What has Thy servant but what he has received from Thee, even without any merit of his own?

All things are Thine, both what Thou hast given and what Thou hast made.

I am poor, and in labours from my youth,[1] and my soul is sometimes sad even to tears; and sometimes too my spirit is disturbed within itself by reason of impending suffering.

2. I desire the joy of peace; I beg earnestly for the peace of Thy children, who are fed by Thee in the light of consolation.

If Thou give peace, if Thou infuse holy joy, the soul of Thy servant shall be full of melody, and devout in Thy praise.

But if Thou withdraw Thyself, as very often Thou art wont to do, he will not be able to run in the way of Thy commandments,[2] but must rather bow down his knees and strike his breast, because it is not with him as yesterday and the day before,[3] when Thy lamp shone over his head,[4] and he was protected under the shadow of Thy wings[5] from assaulting temptations.

3. O just Father, holy, and ever to be praised, the hour is come for Thy servant to be tried.

O Father, worthy of all love, it is fitting that Thy servant should at this hour suffer something for Thee.

O Father, always to be honoured, the hour is come which from all eternity Thou didst foresee would arrive: that Thy servant for a short time should be oppressed outwardly, but inwardly should ever live to Thee; that he should be for a little while slighted and humbled, and should fail in the sight

---

[1] Psalm lxxxvii, 16.
[2] Psalm cxviii, 32.
[3] Genesis xxxi, 2, 5.
[4] Job xxix, 3.
[5] Psalm xvi, 8.

of men; that he should be severely afflicted with sufferings and languors, so that he may rise again with Thee in the dawning of the new day, and be glorified in heaven.

O holy Father, Thou hast so appointed, and such is Thy will; and that has come to pass which Thou hast ordained.

4. For this is a favour to Thy friend, that for Thy love he should suffer and be afflicted in this world, how often soever and by whomsoever Thou shalt permit it to befall him.

Without Thy design and providence, and without cause, there is nothing done upon earth.[1]

It is good for me, O Lord, that Thou hast humbled me, that I may learn Thy justifications,[2] and that I may cast away all pride of heart and presumption.

It is profitable for me that shame has covered my face,[3] that I may seek my consolation from Thee rather than from men.

Hereby also I have learned to dread Thy inscrutable judgements; for Thou dost afflict the just with the wicked, but not without equity and justice.

5. I return Thee thanks that Thou hast not spared my evil ways, but hast bruised me with bitter stripes, inflicting anguish and sending trials, both within and without.

There is none else under heaven that can comfort me but Thou, O Lord my God, the heavenly Physician of souls, who woundest and healest, bringest down to hell and leadest back again.[4]

Thy discipline is upon me, and Thy rod itself shall instruct me.

6. O beloved Father, I am in Thy hands; I bow myself down under the rod of Thy correction.

Strike Thou my back and my neck, that I may bend my crookedness to Thy will.

Make me a true and humble disciple, as Thou art well wont to do, so that I may walk according to Thy every nod.

To Thee I commit myself and all that is mine, for Thy correction. It is better to be chastised here than hereafter.

Thou knowest all things and each thing singly, and nothing in man's conscience is hidden from Thee.

Thou knowest things to come before they happen; and Thou needest no man to teach or warn Thee of what is being done on earth.

Thou knowest what is expedient for my progress, and how greatly tribulation serves to scour off the rust of sin.

[1] Job v, 6.
[2] Psalm cxviii, 71.
[3] Psalm lxviii, 8.
[4] Tobias xiii, 2.

Do with me according to Thy desired good pleasure; and despise not my sinful life, which is known to no one better or more clearly than to Thyself.

7. Grant me, O Lord, to know what I ought to know, to love what I ought to love, to praise what is most pleasing to Thee, to esteem what appears precious to Thee, to abominate what is foul in Thy sight.

Suffer me not to judge according to the sight of the outward eyes, nor to give sentence according to the hearing of the ears of ignorant men; but to determine matters both visible and spiritual with true judgement; and above all things, ever to seek Thy good will and pleasure.

8. Men's minds are often deceived in their judgements; and the lovers of this world are deceived in loving only visible things.

How is a man a whit the better because he is reputed great by men?

When men extol one another, the deceiver cheats the deceiver, the vain man the vain, the blind man the blind, the weak man the weak.

Of a truth a man is put to the greater shame when he receives this vain praise.

For what every one is in Thy sight, so much is he and no more, says the humble Saint Francis.[1]

CHAPTER 51

THAT WE MUST EXERCISE OURSELVES IN HUMBLE WORKS WHEN WE CANNOT ATTAIN TO THE HIGHEST

MY son, you cannot always continue in the more fervent desire of virtue, nor remain constantly in the higher degree of contemplation; but it must needs be that you sometimes, by reason of original corruption, descend to lower things, and bear the burden of this mortal life, even against your will and with weariness.

As long as you carry a mortal body, you shall feel weariness and heaviness of heart.

Therefore, while you are in the flesh, you should often bewail the burden of the flesh, since you cannot unceasingly give yourself to spiritual exercises and divine contemplation.

2. On such occasions it is expedient for you to betake yourself to humble and outward works, and to refresh yourself with

[1] St Bonaventure, *Life of St Francis*, vi.

good deeds; to await My coming and heavenly visitation with
an assured hope; to bear with patience your banishment and
the aridity of your mind, until you be again visited by Me
and freed from all anxieties.

For I will cause you to forget your labours and to enjoy
inward rest.

I will spread open before you the pleasant fields of the
Scriptures, that your heart being enlarged you may begin to
run in the way of My commandments.[1]

And you shall say: *The sufferings of this time are not
worthy to be compared with the glory to come, that shall be
revealed in us.*[2]

CHAPTER 52

THAT A MAN OUGHT TO ESTEEM HIMSELF DESERV-ING OF CHASTISEMENT RATHER THAN WORTHY OF CONSOLATION

O LORD, I am not worthy of Thy consolation, nor of any
spiritual visitation; and therefore Thou dost deal justly with
me when Thou leavest me poor and desolate.

For though I could shed a sea of tears, yet should I not be
worthy of Thy consolation.

Wherefore I deserve nothing else but to be scourged and
punished, because I have grievously and often offended Thee,
and in many things have greatly sinned.

So that, according to right reason, I do not deserve the least
consolation.

But Thou, O gracious and merciful God, who willest not
that Thy works perish, in order to show the riches of Thy
goodness towards the vessels of mercy,[3] dost vouchsafe to console Thy servant, beyond all his desert and above human
measure.

For Thy consolations are not like the vain chatter of men.

2. What have I done, O Lord, that Thou shouldst bestow on
me any heavenly consolations?

I remember that I have done no good; that, on the contrary, I have been ever prone to sin and slow to amend.

This is true and I cannot deny it; if I should say otherwise,
Thou wouldst stand against me, and there would be none to
defend me.

[1] Psalm cxviii, 32.
[2] Romans viii, 18.
[3] Romans ix, 23.

What have I deserved for my sins but hell and everlasting fire?

Truthfully do I confess that I am worthy of all scorn and contempt; neither is it fitting that I should consort with Thy devout servants.

And although it grieves me to hear this, yet for truth's sake I will accuse myself and condemn my sins, that so I may the easier deserve to obtain Thy mercy.

3. What shall I say, guilty as I am and full of all confusion?

My mouth can utter nothing but this one sentence only: I have sinned, O Lord, I have sinned; have mercy on me and pardon me.

Suffer me a little while, that I may lament my sorrow, before I go to a land that is dark and covered with the mist of death.[1]

What dost Thou especially require of a guilty and wretched sinner, but that he should be contrite, and humble himself for his sins?

True contrition and humility of heart give hope of forgiveness; the troubled conscience is reconciled; lost grace is restored; man is secured from the wrath to come; and God and the penitent soul meet together in a holy kiss.

4. Humble contrition for sins is an acceptable sacrifice to Thee, O Lord, far sweeter before Thee than the odour of frankincense.

This is also that pleasant ointment which Thou didst will should be poured upon Thy sacred feet;[2] for a contrite and humbled heart[3] Thou hast never despised.

Here is the place of refuge from the face of the enemy's anger.

Here is amended and washed away whatever defilement has been elsewhere contracted.

CHAPTER 53

THAT THE GRACE OF GOD IS NOT GIVEN TO THE EARTHLY-MINDED

Son, My grace is precious; it does not suffer itself to be mingled with outward things or with earthly consolations.

Therefore, you must cast away every obstacle to grace, if you desire to receive its infusion.

[1] Job x, 20, 21.
[2] Luke vii, 38.
[3] Psalm 1, 19.

Choose for yourself a place apart; love to dwell alone with yourself; seek not the company of any one; but rather pour forth devout prayer to God, that you may keep your mind in compunction and your conscience pure.

Esteem the whole world as nothing; prefer attendance on God before all outward occupations.

For you cannot attend to Me and at the same time take delight in transitory things.

You must sequester yourself from your acquaintances and dear friends, and keep your mind disengaged from all temporal consolation.

Even so the blessed apostle Peter beseeches the faithful of Christ to keep themselves as strangers and pilgrims in this world.[1]

2. O what great confidence shall he have at the hour of death, whom no affection for any earthly thing detains in the world!

But the sickly soul cannot keep its heart thus perfectly disengaged from all things; neither does the natural man understand the liberty of the spiritual man.

But, if he wishes to be truly spiritual, a man must renounce both acquaintances and friends and beware of none more than of himself.

If you perfectly conquer yourself, you shall more easily subdue all other things.

The perfect victory is to triumph over oneself.

For whosoever keeps himself in subjection, so that sensuality obeys reason, and reason is in all things obedient to Me, he is truly conqueror of himself and lord of the world.

3. If you desire to attain this height, you must begin manfully by laying the axe to the root,[2] in order to remove and destroy your secret inordinate attachment to yourself or to any private and material good.

This vice of inordinate self-love is the source of almost everything that has to be radically destroyed. If this evil be vanquished and subdued, there will at once follow great peace and tranquillity.

But because few men strive to die perfectly to themselves, or ever fully transcend themselves, therefore do they remain self-entangled and their souls cannot rise above self to God.

If a man desires to walk freely with Me, he must mortify all his corrupt and inordinate affections and cleave with particular love and desire to no creature whatever.

---

[1] 1 Peter ii, 11.
[2] Matthew iii, 10.

CHAPTER 54

OF THE DIFFERENT MOTIONS OF
NATURE AND GRACE

MY son, observe diligently the motions of nature and grace. They move in ways that are very different yet very subtle, so that they can hardly be distinguished except by a spiritual man and one who is inwardly enlightened.

All men desire the good, and in what they say and do allege some good end; but it happens that many are deceived by a seeming good.

Nature is crafty and draws away many, ensnaring and deceiving them, and always has self for her end.

But grace walks in simplicity, turns aside from every appearance of evil, puts out no false pretences, but does all things purely for God, in whom also she rests as in her last End.

2. Nature is unwilling to die, or to be restrained, or overcome, or made subject; she will not of her own accord come under any yoke.

But grace strives to mortify self, resists sensuality, seeks to be subject, longs to be subdued, has no wish to enjoy her own liberty, loves to be kept under discipline, and desires to have authority over no one. It is her will ever to live, stand, and be under God; and for God's sake she is always ready to submit herself humbly to every human creature.

Nature works for her own advantage, and considers what gain she may derive from another.

But grace does not consider what may be useful and advantageous to herself, but rather what may be profitable to many.

Nature willingly receives honour and respect; but grace faithfully ascribes all honour and glory to God.

3. Nature dreads shame and contempt; but grace rejoices to suffer reproach for the name of Jesus.[1]

Nature loves ease and bodily repose; but grace cannot be idle, and embraces labour gladly.

Nature seeks to have things that are curious and beautiful, and abhors such as are cheap and coarse.

But grace delights in what is plain and humble, does not reject coarse things, or refuse to be clad in old garments.

Nature has its eye on temporal things, rejoices at earthly gains, grieves over losses, and is vexed by a slightly injurious word.

[1] Acts v, 41.

But grace attends to things eternal and cleaves not to temporal things; no hard words exasperate, nor losses disturb her; for she places her joy and treasure in heaven, where nothing is lost.

4. Nature is covetous, and prefers to receive rather than to give; and she loves to have things of her own and private to herself.

But grace is kind and open-hearted, shuns self-interest, is contented with little, and judges it more blessed to give than to receive.[1]

Nature turns a man to creatures, to his own flesh, to vanities, and to much gadding abroad.

But grace draws a man to God and to virtue; she renounces creatures, flies from the world, hates the desires of the flesh, is no gadabout but reluctant to appear in public.

Nature welcomes outward solaces in which her senses may take delight.

But grace seeks consolation in God alone, desiring to pass beyond all visible things and find delight in the Sovereign Good.

5. Nature acts entirely for her own gain and interest. She can do nothing gratis; if she perform a good deed, she hopes to gain something equal or better, or else praise and favour. She is eager to have her deeds and gifts and words highly esteemed.

But grace seeks nothing temporal, nor requires any other recompense than God alone. She desires no more of the necessaries of this life than may serve her to obtain things eternal.

6. Nature rejoices in a multitude of friends and kindred, glories in rank and family, fawns on the powerful, flatters the rich, and applauds those who are like herself.

But grace loves even her enemies and takes no pride in crowds of friends. She sets no store by rank or birth, unless they be joined with greater virtue. She favours the poor rather than the rich; her sympathy is with the innocent rather than with the mighty; she rejoices with him that loves truth, and not with the deceitful; she ever exhorts the good to be zealous for the better gifts,[2] and by the exercise of virtues to become like to the Son of God.

Nature soon complains of want and trouble; but grace bears poverty with constancy.

7. Nature refers all things to herself, and for herself she strives and disputes.

But grace refers all things to God, from whom they take

---

[1] Acts xx, 35.
[2] 1 Corinthians xii, 31.

their origin; she ascribes no good to herself, nor arrogantly presumes on herself.

Grace does not contend, or prefer her own opinion, but in every matter of thought or reason submits herself wholly to the Eternal Wisdom and to His judgement.

Nature is eager to know secrets and to hear news; she likes to be seen abroad and to experience many things by her own senses; she longs to be noticed, and to do such things as may procure praise and admiration.

But grace cares not for the hearing of things new and curious, because all this springs from man's old corruption, nor is there anything new or lasting upon the earth.[1]

Grace teaches, therefore, that we should restrain the senses, avoid vain complacency and ostentation, humbly hide those things which are worthy of praise and admiration, and from every thing and in all knowledge seek profitable fruit, and the praise and honour of God.

Grace does not desire that herself, or what belongs to her, should be extolled; but recognizes the gifts of God and desires that He should be blessed, who out of mere love bestows all things upon us.

8. This grace is a supernatural light and a certain special gift of God, the proper mark of the elect, and the pledge of eternal salvation. It elevates a man from the things of the earth to the love of heavenly things, and makes him spiritual who before was carnal.

Therefore, the more nature is kept down and subdued, the greater is the grace that is infused; and day by day, by new visitations, is the spiritual man reformed according to the pattern proposed by God.[2]

CHAPTER 55

OF THE CORRUPTION OF NATURE, AND OF THE EFFICACY OF DIVINE GRACE

O LORD my God, who hast created me to Thine own image and likeness, grant me this grace which Thou hast shown to be so great and so necessary for salvation, in order that I may overcome my most wicked nature, which draws me to sin and to perdition.

For I perceive in my flesh the law of sin contradicting the

[1] Ecclesiastes i, 10.
[2] 2 Corinthians iv, 16; Colossians iii, 10.

law of my mind and leading me captive in many ways to sensuality.

Neither can I resist the passions of the flesh, unless I be assisted by Thy most holy grace and my heart be enkindled by its visitation.

2. I stand in need of Thy grace, and of great grace, in order to overcome nature, which from earliest youth is ever prone to evil.[1]

For in Adam, the first man, nature fell and was corrupted by sin. And the penalty of that stain has descended upon all mankind, so that nature itself, which by Thee was created good and right, now commonly denotes vice and infirmity, since our fallen nature, when left to itself, tends to evil and things that are base.

The little strength which it retains is like a spark hidden in ashes.

This spark is our natural reason, which though encompassed with much darkness is yet able to judge between good and evil, and to discern truth and falsehood. It is unable, however, to fulfil all that it approves, for it no longer possesses the full light of truth and its affections are impaired.

3. Hence it is, O my God, that according to the inward man I delight in Thy law,[2] knowing that Thy commandment will be good, just, and holy, and that it also reproves all evil and sin, as things to be shunned.

And yet in the flesh I serve the law of sin,[3] obeying sensuality rather than reason.

Hence it is, that I have the intention to do what is good and yet fail to fulfil that intention.[4]

Hence I often make many good resolutions, but meeting with some slight resistance recoil and fail, because I lack the grace that would help my weakness.

Hence it comes to pass that I know the way of perfection, and see clearly enough what I ought to do, but pressed down with the weight of my own corruption, I rise not to the things that are more perfect.

4. O Lord, how supremely necessary for me is Thy grace, so that I may begin what is good, go forward with it, and accomplish it!

For without it I can do nothing;[5] but I can do all things in Thee, when grace strengthens me.[6]

---

[1] Genesis viii, 21.
[2] Romans vii, 12-25.
[3] *Loc. cit.*
[4] Romans vii, 18.
[5] John xv, 5.
[6] Philippians iv, 13.

O grace truly celestial, without which our own merits are worth nothing, neither are the gifts of nature to be esteemed!

Neither talents nor wealth, neither beauty nor strength, neither wit nor eloquence have any value in Thy sight, O Lord, without grace.

For the gifts of nature are common to good and bad; but grace is the special gift of the elect; and they that are adorned with it are deemed worthy of eternal life.

This grace is so excellent that neither the gift of prophecy, nor the working of miracles, nor the most sublime speculation is of any account without it.

No, not even faith, or hope, or any other virtues are acceptable to Thee without charity and grace.

5. O most blessed grace, which makes the poor in spirit rich in virtues, and renders him humble of heart, for all his blessings! Come, descend upon me, and replenish me soon with Thy consolation, lest my soul faint for weariness and aridity of mind.

I beseech Thee, O Lord, that I may find grace in Thine eyes; for Thy grace is sufficient for me,[1] though I obtain none of those things which nature desires.

Though I be tempted and afflicted with many tribulations, I will fear no evils, so long as Thy grace is with me.[2]

This alone is my strength, this alone brings counsel and help.

This is more mighty than all enemies, and wiser than all the wise.

6. Thy grace is the mistress of truth, the teacher of discipline, the light of the heart, the consoler of anguish, the banisher of sorrow, the expeller of fear, the nurse of devotion, the producer of tears.

What am I without this grace but a dry tree and an unprofitable branch, fit only to be cast away?

Therefore, *O Lord, let Thy grace always go before me and follow me, and make me ever intent upon good works, through Jesus Christ Thy Son. Amen.*[3]

[1] 2 Corinthians xii, 9.
[2] Psalm xxii, 4.
[3] Sixteenth Sunday after Pentecost, the Collect.

CHAPTER 56

THAT WE OUGHT TO DENY OURSELVES AND IMITATE CHRIST BY THE CROSS

MY son, in proportion as you can go out of yourself, so will you be able to enter into Me.

Just as the desiring no outward thing brings inward peace, so does the forsaking of yourself inwardly bring union with God.

I will have you learn the perfect renunciation of yourself to My will, without contradiction or complaint.

Follow Me: *I am the way, the truth, and the life.*[1]

Without the way there is no going; without the truth there is no knowing; without the life there is no living.

I am the way which you should follow, the truth which you should believe, the life which you should hope for.

I am the way inviolable, the truth infallible, the life everlasting.

I am the straightest way, the sovereign truth, the true life, the blessed life, the uncreated life.

2. If you abide in My way, you shall know the truth, and the truth shall make you free,[2] and you shall attain to life everlasting.

If you will enter into life, keep the commandments.[3]

If you will know the truth, believe Me: if you will be perfect, sell all.[4]

If you will be My disciple, deny yourself.[5]

If you will possess the blessed life, despise this present life.

If you will be exalted in heaven, humble yourself in this world.

If you will reign with Me, bear the cross with Me.[6]

For none but the servants of the cross find the way of bliss and true light.

3. O Lord Jesus, since Thy own way was strait and despised by the world, grant that I may follow Thee, though with the world's contempt.

[1] John xiv, 6.
[2] John viii, 31, 32.
[3] Matthew xix, 17.
[4] Matthew xix, 21.
[5] Luke ix, 23.
[6] *Loc. Cit.*

For the servant is not greater than his lord, neither is the disciple above his master.[1]

Let Thy servant be exercised in Thy life, for there is my salvation and true holiness.

Whatever else I read or hear does not refresh or fully delight me.

4. My son, since you know these things and have read them all, you shall be blessed if you do them.[2]

He that has My commandments and keeps them, he it is that loves Me. And I will love him, and will manifest Myself unto him,[3] and will make him sit with Me in the kingdom of My Father.[4]

Lord Jesus, as Thou hast said and hast promised, so let it be indeed, and may it be my lot to merit it.

I have received the cross, I have received it from Thy hand, I will bear it, and bear it even to death, as Thou hast laid it upon me.

Truly the life of a good monk is a cross; but it leads him to paradise.

We have begun; we may not go back; neither should we abandon our purpose.

5. Take courage, brethren; let us go forward together; Jesus will be with us.

For the sake of Jesus we have taken up this cross; for Jesus' sake let us persevere in the cross.

He will be our Helper, who is our Captain and our Forerunner.

Lo, our King marches before us and He will fight for us.[5]

Let us follow Him like men; let no one fear any terrors; let us be ready to die valiantly in battle; and let us not stain our glory by flying from the cross.

[1] Matthew x, 24; Luke vi, 40.
[2] John xiii, 17.
[3] John xiv, 21.
[4] Apocalypse iii, 21.
[5] 2 Esdras iv, 20.

CHAPTER 57

THAT A MAN SHOULD NOT BE TOO MUCH DEJECTED WHEN HE FALLS INTO SOME DEFECTS

My son, patience and humility in adversity please me more than much consolation and devotion in prosperity.

Why are you afflicted at a little word spoken against you?

Even had it been more, you ought not to have been disturbed.

But now let it pass. It is not the first attack, or anything new; nor will it be the last, if you live long.

You are valiant enough, so long as no adversity comes your way.

You can also give good counsel, and know how to encourage others with your words.

But, when an unexpected tribulation comes to your own door, then your counsel and your courage fail you.

Consider your great frailty, of which you often have experience in trifling difficulties. Nevertheless, when these or similar trials come to you, they befall you for your salvation.

2. To the best of your ability, put the tribulation out of your heart; and if it have affected you, yet let it not cast you down, or long embarrass you.

If you cannot bear it gladly, at least bear it patiently.

And although disagreeable things be said of you and you feel indignant, yet hold yourself in check, and take care that you utter no inordinate word, whereby scandal may be given to little ones.

A storm has been raised; but it shall quickly be allayed, and your inward grief shall be sweetened by returning grace.

I still live, says the Lord, and am ready to help you more than before, provided that you put your trust in Me and devoutly call upon Me.

3. Be of good heart, and gird yourself to yet greater endurance.

Although you often find yourself afflicted or grievously tempted, all is not lost.

You are a man and not a god; you are flesh and not an angel.

Perseverance failed Lucifer in heaven, and likewise Adam in paradise. How then might you continue always in the selfsame state of virtue?

I am He who raises up and rescues those that mourn; and when men recognize their weakness, I promote them to a share in My divinity.

4. O Lord, blessed be Thy word; it is sweeter to my mouth than honey and the honeycomb.[1]

What should I do in my great tribulations and trials, didst Thou not strengthen me with Thy holy words?

Provided only that I reach at last the haven of salvation, what matter how many or how great trials I endure?

Grant me a good end, grant me a happy passage out of this world.

Be mindful of me, O my God, and direct me in the right road to Thy Kingdom. Amen.

CHAPTER 58

OF NOT SEARCHING INTO HIGH MATTERS OR INTO THE SECRET JUDGEMENTS OF GOD

My son, beware of disputing about high matters and the hidden judgements of God. Ask not why this man is so forsaken, and that other raised to so great grace; or why this person is so much afflicted, and that other so highly exalted.

Such things exceed all human comprehension, nor can any reasoning or disputation fathom the inscrutable judgements of God.

When, therefore, the enemy suggests such things to you, or certain curious men inquire into them, answer with the prophet: *Thou art just, O Lord, and Thy judgement is right.*[2] And again: *The judgements of the Lord are true, justified in themselves.*[3]

My judgements are to be feared, not to be discussed; for they are incomprehensible to human understanding.

2. In like manner, do not inquire or dispute concerning the merits of the Saints: which of them is holier than another, or which greater in the Kingdom of Heaven.

Such questions often breed strife and unprofitable contention, and nourish also pride and vainglory; whence arise envies and dissensions, while one man proudly prefers this Saint and another that.

Curiosity about such matters and inquiry into them are unprofitable, serving only to displease the Saints. For I am

[1] Psalm xviii, 11; cxviii, 103.
[2] Psalm cxviii, 137.
[3] Psalm xviii, 10.

not the God of dissension but of peace; which peace consists rather in true humility than in self-exaltation.

3. Some in their zealous love are attracted to these Saints or those with a greater affection; but this affection is more human than divine.

I am He who made all the Saints; I gave them grace and I have granted them glory. I know the merits of each; I forestalled them with the blessings of My sweetness.[1] I foreknew My beloved ones before all ages.[2] I chose them out of the world; they did not first choose Me.[3]

I called them by grace;[4] I drew them by mercy;[5] I brought them safe through many temptations; I poured upon them abundant consolations; I gave them perseverance; I have crowned their patience.

4. I know who is first and who last; I embrace all alike with an inestimable love.

I am to be praised in all My Saints;[6] I am always to be blessed above all, and to be honoured in each, whom I have so gloriously magnified and predestinated, without any fore-going merits of their own.

He, therefore, that despises one of My least ones,[7] does not honour the greatest; for I have made them all, both little and great.

And he that disparages any one of the Saints, disparages Me also, and all others in the Kingdom of Heaven.

They are all one through the bond of charity; their thought is the same; their will is the same; and all are united in love, one for another.

5. But what is a far higher thing, they love Me more than themselves or any merits of their own.

For, rapt above themselves, and utterly drawn away from self-love, they plunge wholly into the love of Me, and rest in the fruition of that love.

Nothing can retard or suppress them; for being full of the eternal Truth, they burn with the fire of unquenchable charity.

Therefore, let carnal and sensual men, who are unable to love anything but their own selfish pleasures, be silent upon the subject of the state of the Saints. They exalt or depreciate their condition according to their own likes or dislikes, and not according to the mind of Eternal Truth.

---

[1] Psalm xx, 4.
[2] Romans viii, 29.
[3] John xv, 16, 19.
[4] Galatians i, 15.
[5] Jeremias xxxi, 3.
[6] Psalm cl, 1.
[7] Matthew xviii, 10.

6. In the case of many, it is just ignorance. And this is especially true of those who are but little enlightened and can seldom love any one with a perfect spiritual love.

They are as yet much inclined, by natural affection and human friendship, to this man or that; and according to their practice in mundane matters, just such are their imaginations regarding the things of heaven.

But between the notions of these imperfect folk and the heavenly revelations that come to enlightened men, the distance is beyond measure.

7. Take heed therefore, My son, that you treat not too curiously of those things which exceed your knowledge; but let this be your business and aim: that you be found, though it be but the least, in the Kingdom of God.

Even should a man know who was holier than another, or accounted greater in the Kingdom of Heaven, what would this knowledge profit him, unless it made him humble himself in My sight, and rise to give the greater praise to My Name.

That man is much more acceptable to God who thinks of the greatness of his sins and the smallness of his virtues, and how far he is from the perfection of the Saints, than he who disputes which of them is the greater, which the less.

It is better to supplicate the Saints with devout prayers and tears, and with a humble mind to implore their glorious intercession, than to search with vain curiosity into their secrets.

8. They themselves are fully and perfectly contented. O that men could be content likewise and abstain from their vain discussions!

The Saints glory not in their own merits; for they ascribe none of their virtues to themselves but all to Me, who of My infinite love have given them all things.

They are filled with so great a love of the Godhead, and with joy so overflowing, that no glory is wanting to them, nor can anything be lacking to their happiness.

The higher they are in glory, so much the humbler are all the Saints in themselves, and nearer to Me, and more beloved by Me.

And therefore you have it written, that *they cast down their crowns before God, and fell on their faces before the Lamb, and adored Him that lives for ever and ever.*[1]

There are many that ask who is the greater in the Kingdom of God, and themselves know not whether they shall be worthy to be numbered among the least.

[1] Apocalypse iv, 10; v, 14.

9. It is a great thing to be even the least in heaven, where all are great; because all shall be called and shall be the sons of God.[1]

The least shall become a thousand; the sinner a hundred years old shall die.[2]

When the disciples asked, who was the greater in the Kingdom of Heaven, they received this answer:

Unless you be converted, and become as little children, you shall not enter into the Kingdom of Heaven. Whosoever, therefore, shall humble himself as this little child, he is the greater in the Kingdom of Heaven.[3]

10. Woe to them who disdain to humble themselves willingly with little children; because the lowly gate of the heavenly Kingdom will not allow them to enter.

Woe also to the rich, who have their consolations here.[4] For when the poor enter into the Kingdom of God, they shall stand lamenting without.

Rejoice, ye humble, and be glad, ye poor, for yours is the Kingdom of God;[5] if at least you walk in the truth.[6]

CHAPTER 59

THAT ALL OUR HOPE AND CONFIDENCE SHOULD
BE FIXED IN GOD ALONE

LORD, what is my hope here in this life? or what is my greatest solace amongst all the things that are seen under heaven?

Is it not Thou, my Lord God, of whose mercy there is no number?

When has it ever been well with me without Thee? or when could it be ill with me when Thou wast present?

I had rather be poor for Thy sake than rich without Thee.

I had rather be a pilgrim upon earth with Thee than possess heaven without Thee.

Where Thou art, there is heaven; and where Thou art not, there are death and hell.

Thou art my desire, and therefore I must needs sigh after Thee, and cry and pray.

[1] Matthew v, 9; 1 John iii, 1.
[2] Isaias lx, 22; lxv, 20.
[3] Matthew xviii, 3, 4.
[4] Luke vi, 24.
[5] Matthew v, 3.
[6] 2 John 4.

There is none save Thee, my God, whom I can trust to bring me true help in my necessities.

Thou art my hope, my confidence, my comforter, and in all things most faithful.

2. All seek the things that are their own;[1] Thou aimest only at my salvation and profit, and turnest all things to my good.

Although Thou expose me to divers temptations and adversities, yet all this Thou dost ordain for my good, who art wont to prove Thy beloved servants in a thousand ways.

Under which probation Thou shouldst be no less loved and praised than if Thou wert filling me with heavenly consolations.

3. In Thee, therefore, O Lord God, do I place all my hope and confidence; on Thee I rest all my tribulation and anguish; for I find all things to be weak and inconstant, whatsoever I behold apart from Thee.

For neither will many friends be of service to me, nor can powerful helpers assist me, nor wise counsellors give me a profitable answer, nor the books of the learned give me consolation, nor any precious substance ransom me, nor any secret and lovely place shelter me, if Thou Thyself do not assist me, and do not help, strengthen, comfort, instruct and guard me.

4. For, when Thou art absent, all things which seem to be for our peace and happiness are worth nothing, and in truth confer no happiness.

Thou, therefore, art the perfection of all good, the summit of life, and the depth of wisdom; and to trust in Thee above all things is the strongest comfort of Thy servants.

Unto Thee do I lift up mine eyes; in Thee, O my God, Father of mercies, do I put my trust.[2]

Bless and sanctify my soul with heavenly benediction, that it may become Thy holy habitation and the seat of Thy eternal glory; and let nothing be found in the temple of Thy dignity that may offend the eyes of Thy Majesty.

According to the greatness of Thy goodness and the multitude of Thy tender mercies[3] look down upon me, and give ear to the prayer of Thy poor servant, a far-distant exile in the region of the shadow of death.[4]

Protect and preserve the soul of Thy poor servant amidst the many perils of this corruptible life, and by Thy accompanying grace direct him along the path of peace to his native country of everlasting light. Amen.

[1] Philippians ii, 21.
[2] Psalm cxxii, 1; x, 2; 2 Corinthians i, 3.
[3] Psalm 1, 3.
[4] Isaias ix, 2.

THE FOURTH BOOK

A DEVOUT EXHORTATION
TO HOLY COMMUNION

THE VOICE OF CHRIST

*Come to Me, all you that labour and are burdened and
I will refresh you,* says the Lord.[1]

*The bread that I will give is My flesh, for the life of
the world.*[2]

*Take ye and eat; this is My body, which shall be delivered
for you.*[3] *Do this for the commemoration of Me.*[4]

*He that eats My flesh and drinks My blood, abides in Me,
and I in him.*

The words that I have spoken to you are spirit and life.[5]

CHAPTER 1

WITH HOW GREAT REVERENCE CHRIST
OUGHT TO BE RECEIVED

THE VOICE OF THE DISCIPLE

THESE are Thy words, O Christ, the eternal Truth, though
not all uttered at one time, nor written in one place.

Since, therefore, they are Thine and true, they ought all
to be received by me thankfully and faithfully.

They are Thine, and Thou didst utter them; and they are
also mine, because Thou didst speak them for my salvation.

I willingly receive them from Thy mouth, that they may
be the more firmly implanted in my heart.

Words of so great tenderness, so full of sweetness and love,
encourage me; but my own sins terrify me, and an unclean
conscience keeps me back from receiving so great Mysteries.
The sweetness of Thy words beckons me onwards; but the
multitude of my sins weighs me down.

2. Thou commandest me to approach to Thee with confidence, if I would have part with Thee; and to receive the

---

[1] Matthew xi, 28.
[2] John vi, 51.
[3] Matthew xxvi, 26.
[4] 1 Corinthians xi, 24.
[5] John vi, 56, 64.

food of immortality, if I desire to obtain everlasting life and glory.

Come to Me, sayest Thou, *all you that labour and are burdened, and I will refresh you.*

O sweet and loving word in the ear of a sinner, that Thou, O Lord my God, dost invite the poor and needy to the Communion of Thy most holy Body!

But who am I, O Lord, that I should presume to approach unto Thee?

The heaven of heavens cannot contain Thee;[1] and Thou sayest, *Come ye all to Me.*

3. What is the meaning of this most loving condescension and so friendly invitation?

How shall I dare to approach, who am conscious to myself of no good on which I can presume?

How shall I bring Thee into my house,[2] who have too often offended Thy most gracious countenance?

Angels and Archangels stand in awe of Thee; the Saints and the just are afraid; and Thou sayest, *Come ye all to Me.*

Unless Thou, O Lord, didst say this, who would believe it to be true?

And unless Thou didst command it, who would venture to approach?

4. Behold, Noah, that just man, laboured a hundred years in building the ark, that with a few he might be saved: and how can I in the space of one hour prepare myself to receive with reverence the Maker of the world?

Moses, Thy great servant and special friend, made an Ark of incorruptible wood, which also he covered with most pure gold, that he might deposit therein the Tables of the Law: and I, a corrupted creature, shall I presume so easily to receive Thee, the Maker of the Law and the Giver of life?

Solomon, the wisest of the kings of Israel, spent seven years in building a magnificent temple for the praise of Thy Name, and for eight days he celebrated the feast of its dedication; he offered a thousand peace-making victims, and solemnly set the Ark of the Covenant in the place prepared for it, with sound of trumpet and rejoicing: and I, unhappy and poorest of men, how shall I bring Thee into my house, who can hardly spend one half-hour devoutly? And would that I might even spend as much as one half-hour worthily!

5. O my God, how much did they endeavour to do to please Thee! Alas, how little it is that I do! How short a time do I spend when I prepare myself to communicate!

[1] 3 Kings viii, 27.
[2] Canticle of Canticles iii, 4.

Seldom am I wholly recollected; very seldom am I free from all distraction.

And yet, surely, in the life-giving presence of Thy Godhead, no unbecoming thought should intrude, nor anything created occupy my mind; for it is not an Angel, but the Lord of Angels, whom I am about to entertain as my guest.

6. And yet there is a very great difference between the Ark of the Covenant with its relics, and Thy most pure Body with its unspeakable virtues; between those sacrifices of the Law, which were figures of things to come, and the true Sacrifice of Thy Body, which is the accomplishment of all the ancient sacrifices.

Why, then, do I not seek Thy adorable presence with greater fervour?

Why do I not prepare myself with greater solicitude to receive Thy sacred gifts, seeing that those ancient holy Patriarchs and Prophets, yes, kings also and princes, with the whole people, manifested so great devotion towards Thy divine worship?

7. The most devout king David danced with all his might before the Ark of God, as he called to mind the benefits in times past bestowed upon the fathers; he made musical instruments of various kinds; he composed psalms, and appointed them to be sung with joy; and he himself likewise often sang them to his harp, inspired with the grace of the Holy Spirit. He taught the people of Israel to praise God with their whole heart, and with one concordant voice to bless Him and proclaim Him every day.

If so great devotion was then displayed before the Ark of the Covenant, and so great a celebration there performed to the praise of God, how great should be the veneration and devotion of myself and all Christian people in the presence of this Sacrament and at the reception of the most precious Body of Christ?

8. Many run to sundry places to visit the shrines of the Saints. They wonder to hear of their deeds and to gaze upon the spacious buildings of their churches; and they behold and kiss their bones, all wrapped in silks and gold.

And lo! Thou Thyself art here present to me on the altar, my God, the Saint of Saints, the Creator of men, and the Lord of Angels.

Often such pilgrims as these are moved by human curiosity and the quest of novelty, and carry home with them small fruit of amendment; especially when they run so gaily from place to place without true contrition.

But here, in the Sacrament of the Altar, Thou art wholly

present, my God, the Man Christ Jesus. And here is reaped in abundance the fruit of eternal salvation, as often as Thou art worthily and devoutly received.

Nor are we in this case drawn by any levity, or curiosity, or sensuality, but by a firm faith, a devout hope, and a sincere charity.

9. O God, unseen Creator of the world, how wonderfully dost Thou deal with us! How sweetly and graciously dost Thou order all things for Thy elect, to whom Thou dost offer Thyself to be received in this Sacrament!

For this passes all understanding; this especially attracts the hearts of the devout and enkindles their love.

For they, Thy true faithful ones, who dispose their whole life to amendment, frequently receive from this most venerable Sacrament a great grace of devotion and love of virtue.

10. O admirable and hidden grace of the Sacrament! which only the faithful of Christ know, but unbelievers, and such as are slaves to sin, cannot experience.

In this Sacrament is conferred spiritual grace; virtue lost is again restored to the soul; and beauty disfigured by sin returns again.

So great sometimes is this grace, that from the fulness of the devotion conferred, not only the mind, but the frail body also, feels an increase of strength bestowed upon it.

11. Yet must we exceedingly lament and deplore our lukewarmness and negligence, that we are not drawn with greater affection to receive Christ, in whom consist all the hope and merit of those that are to be saved.

For He Himself is our sanctification and our redemption; He Himself is the consolation of us earthly wayfarers, and the eternal fruition of the Saints.

Therefore is it greatly to be lamented that many take so little heed of this saving Mystery, which rejoices heaven and preserves the whole world.

Alas for the blindness and hardness of the human heart, that does not more regard so unspeakable a gift, but through daily use even falls into a disregard of it!

12. For if this most holy Sacrament were celebrated in one place only, and consecrated by only one Priest in the world, with how great a desire, think you, would men be affected towards that place and to such a Priest of God, that they might see the Divine Mysteries celebrated?

But now there are many Priests, and Christ is offered up in many places, that the grace and love of God to man may appear so much the greater, the more widely is this Sacred Communion spread throughout the world.

Thanks be to Thee, O good Jesus, eternal Shepherd, who hast vouchsafed to refresh us poor exiles with Thy precious Body and Blood, and to invite us to the receiving of these Mysteries even by the words of Thy own mouth, saying, *Come to Me, all you that labour and are burdened, and I will refresh you.*

CHAPTER 2

THAT THE GREAT GOODNESS AND LOVE OF GOD ARE SHOWN TO MEN IN THIS SACRAMENT

THE VOICE OF THE DISCIPLE

TRUSTING, O Lord, in Thy goodness and in Thy great mercy, I come sick to my Saviour, hungry and thirsty to the Fountain of life, needy to the King of heaven, a servant to my Lord, a creature to my Creator, and one in desolation to my loving Comforter.

But whence is this to me, that Thou shouldst come to me?[1] who am I that Thou shouldst give me Thyself?

How dare a sinner appear before Thee? and how dost Thou vouchsafe to come to a sinner?

Thou knowest Thy servant, and dost know that he has in himself no good thing for which Thou shouldst bestow this boon upon him.

Therefore I confess my unworthiness; I acknowledge Thy goodness; I praise Thy tender mercy; and I give Thee thanks for Thy exceeding love.

For Thou dost this on Thy own account, and not for any merits of mine. Thou wouldst have Thy goodness made more manifest to me, Thy love more abundantly imparted, and Thy humility more perfectly commended.

Since therefore this is Thy pleasure and Thou hast ordained it thus, Thy merciful condescension pleases me also; and O that my wickedness may be no obstacle!

2. O sweetest and kindest Jesus, how great reverence and thanksgiving, together with perpetual praise, are due to Thee for the receiving of Thy sacred Body, whose worthiness no man can be found able to express!

But on what shall I think at this Communion when I approach to my Lord, whom I can never duly venerate, and yet desire to receive with devotion?

What better or more salutary thought can I have, than to

[1] Luke i, 43.

humble myself entirely before Thee, and extol Thy infinite goodness above me?

I praise Thee, O my Lord, and I extol Thee for ever; I despise myself, and cast myself before Thee into the depths of my own vileness.

3. Lo, Thou art the Holy of holies, and I am the scum of sinners.

Lo, Thou bowest Thyself down to me, who am not worthy to look up to Thee.

Lo, Thou comest to me; Thou wishest to be with me; Thou invitest me to Thy banquet; Thou desirest to give me heavenly food and the Bread of Angels to eat. And this, indeed, is nought else than Thyself, the living Bread, who didst come down from heaven and givest life to the world.

4. Behold love's revelation! Behold the glory of this condescension! How great thanks and praise do we not owe Thee for these gifts!

O how salutary and profitable was Thy design when Thou didst institute this Sacrament! How sweet and delightful is this banquet, wherein Thou didst give us Thine own Self to be our food.

O how admirable is Thy work, O Lord! how mighty is Thy power! how infallible Thy truth!

For Thou didst speak, and all things were made; Thou didst command, and this thing was done.

5. A wondrous thing it is, and worthy of faith, and transcending all human understanding, that Thou, O Lord my God, true God and true Man, art contained entire under the lowly appearances of bread and wine, art eaten by the receiver, and art not consumed.

Thou, O Lord of all, who hast need of none, art pleased to dwell within us by means of this Thy Sacrament.

Keep my heart and my body without stain, that I may often be able, with a pure and joyful conscience, to celebrate Thy Sacred Mysteries, and for my eternal salvation to receive that Sacrament, which Thou didst ordain and institute for Thine own especial honour and for a never-ending memorial.

6. Rejoice, O my soul, and give thanks unto God for so noble a gift, and so singular a solace left to you in this valley of tears.

For, as often as you celebrate this Mystery and receive the Body of Christ, so often do you perform the work of your redemption,[1] and are made partaker of the merits of Christ.

For the charity of Christ is never diminished, nor the greatness of His propitiation ever exhausted.

[1] Secret of the Ninth Sunday after Pentecost.

Therefore ought you to dispose yourself for this Sacrament by a constant renewal of your spirit, ever pondering with attentive mind the great mystery of salvation.

And, as often as you celebrate or hear Mass, it ought to seem to you as great, new, and delightful, as if that same day Christ were for the first time descending into the Virgin's womb and becoming Man; or, hanging on the cross, were that day suffering and dying for man's salvation.

CHAPTER 3

THAT IT IS PROFITABLE TO COMMUNICATE OFTEN

THE VOICE OF THE DISCIPLE

I COME to Thee, O Lord, that by Thy gift it may be well with me, and that I may be gladdened by Thy holy banquet, which Thou, O God, in Thy sweetness hast prepared for the poor.[1]

Lo, in Thee is all that I can or ought to desire; Thou art my salvation and redemption, my hope and my strength, my honour and my glory.

Therefore gladden the soul of Thy servant [2] this day, because unto Thee, O Lord Jesus, have I lifted up my soul.

Now do I desire to receive Thee devoutly and reverently; I long to bring Thee into my house, so that with Zaccheus I may deserve to be blessed by Thee, and to be numbered amongst the children of Abraham.[3]

My soul longs eagerly to receive Thy Body; my heart desires to be united with Thee.

2. Give Thyself to me and it is enough; for without Thee no consolation is of any avail.

Without Thee I cannot exist; and without Thy visitation I am unable to live.

Therefore must I often come to Thee, and receive Thee as the medicine of my salvation, lest perchance I faint in the way, if I be deprived of this heavenly food.

For so, O most merciful Jesus, when preaching to the people and healing their many diseases, Thou didst once say: *I will not send them fasting to their homes, lest they faint in the way.*[4]

[1] Psalm lxvii, 11.
[2] Psalm lxxxv, 4.
[3] Luke xix, 9.
[4] Matthew xv, 32.

Deal with me, therefore, in like manner, who hast left Thyself in this Sacrament for the consolation of the Faithful.

For Thou art the sweet refection of the soul, and he that shall eat Thee worthily shall be partaker and heir of everlasting glory.

Necessary, indeed, is it for me, who so often fall and commit sin, so quickly grow torpid and faint, that by frequent prayers and confessions, and by the devout receiving of Thy Body, I renew, cleanse and enkindle my soul, lest perchance by too long abstaining I fall away from my holy purpose.

3. For the senses of man are prone to evil from his youth;[1] and unless the divine medicine succour him, he quickly falls away.

Holy Communion, therefore, withdraws us from evil and strengthens us in good.

For if now I am so often negligent and lukewarm, whenever I communicate or celebrate, what would I be if I did not take this remedy, and did not seek so great a help?

And although every day I be not fit nor in due dispositions for the celebration of Mass, yet I will endeavour at fitting times to receive the Divine Mysteries, and to present myself as a partaker of this great grace.

For herein lies the one chief consolation of a faithful soul, as long as she sojourns far from Thee in this mortal body, that mindful of her God she should often devoutly receive her Beloved.

4. O wondrous condescension towards us of Thy tender mercy![2] that Thou, O Lord God, the Creator and the Life of every spirit, shouldst deign to come to a poor little soul and to feast her famishing hunger with the rich food of Thy whole Divinity and Humanity.

O happy mind and blessed soul! which is counted worthy to receive Thee, her Lord God, with devotion, and in receiving Thee to be filled with spiritual joy.

O how great a Lord does she entertain! how beloved a Guest does she harbour! how sweet a Companion does she receive! how faithful a Friend does she welcome! how beautiful and noble a Spouse does she embrace! even Him who is to be loved beyond all that are beloved, and above all things that can be desired.

O my most sweet Beloved! let heaven and earth and all their furniture be silent before Thy face. There is no glory and no beauty that they possess which is not all the gift of Thy condescending bounty; nor shall they attain to the beauty of Thy Name, for of Thy Wisdom there is no number.[3]

[1] Genesis viii, 21.   [2] From the *Exsultet*.
[3] Psalm cxlvi, 5.

CHAPTER 4

THAT MANY BENEFITS ARE BESTOWED ON THOSE WHO COMMUNICATE DEVOUTLY

THE VOICE OF THE DISCIPLE

O LORD my God, forestall Thy servant with the blessings of Thy sweetness,[1] that I may deserve to approach worthily and devoutly to Thy glorious Sacrament.

Raise up my heart towards Thee, and deliver me from the torpor of sloth.

Visit me with Thy salvation,[2] that I may taste in spirit that sweetness of Thine, which lies copiously hidden in this Sacrament as in its source.

Enlighten also my eyes to behold so great a Mystery, and grant me strength to believe it with an undoubting faith.

For it is Thy work, not the power of man; Thy sacred institution, not man's invention.

For no man is found able of himself to comprehend and understand these things, which transcend even the intelligence of the Angels.

What then shall I, an unworthy sinner, who am but dust and ashes, be able to investigate or comprehend concerning so high and holy a Mystery?

2. O Lord, in the simplicity of my heart, with a good and firm faith, and at Thy command, I come to Thee with hope and reverence; and I do verily believe that Thou art here present in the Sacrament, both God and Man.

Thou willest, then, that I receive Thee and unite myself to Thee in charity.

Wherefore I beseech Thy clemency, and beg of Thee to give me Thy special grace, so that I may be wholly absorbed in Thee and filled with Thy love, and no more concern myself about any other kind of consolation.

For this most high and most worthy Sacrament is the health of soul and body, the medicine of every spiritual malady. By It my vices are cured, my passions restrained, my temptations overcome or lessened; greater grace is infused, incipient virtue increased, faith confirmed, hope strengthened, and charity enkindled and enlarged.

[1] Psalm xx, 4.
[2] Psalm cv, 4.

3. For in this Sacrament Thou hast bestowed and still dost often bestow many good things on Thy beloved ones who communicate devoutly, O my God, the Support of my soul, the Repairer of human infirmity, and the Giver of all interior consolation.

For Thou dost impart to them much consolation against their various tribulations, and Thou liftest them up from the depth of their own abasement to the hope of Thy protection; and Thou dost inwardly refresh and enlighten them with a certain new grace, so that they who first were anxious and without sensible affection before Communion, after being fed with this heavenly Food and Drink do find themselves changed for the better.

And Thou art pleased to deal thus with Thy elect, so that they may more plainly experience and truly acknowledge how great is their weakness when left to themselves, and how much of bounty and grace they receive from Thee.

For of themselves they are cold, dry, and indevout; but by Thee they merit to become fervent, eager, and devout.

For who is there that humbly approaching a sweet fountain does not carry thence some little sweetness?

Or who, standing by a great fire, does not derive therefrom some little heat?

And Thou art a Fountain ever full and overflowing; Thou art a Fire always burning and never failing.

4. Wherefore, if I may not draw from the fulness of the fountain, nor drink my fill, I will at least set my lips to the mouth of this heavenly spring, that so I may catch some little drop to allay my thirst, and may not wholly wither away.

And if as yet I cannot be all heavenly, nor all on fire like the Cherubim and Seraphim, I will still endeavour to pursue devotion and to prepare my heart, that so I may acquire some small spark of the divine fire by humbly receiving this life-giving Sacrament.

And whatever is wanting to me, O good Jesus, most holy Saviour, do Thou in Thy bounty and goodness supply, who hast vouchsafed to call us all to Thee, saying: *Come to Me, all you that labour and are burdened, and I will refresh you.*[1]

5. I labour, indeed, in the sweat of my brow,[2] I am tortured with grief of heart, I am burdened with sins, I am troubled with temptations, I am entangled and oppressed with many evil passions; and there is no one to help me, no one to deliver and save me, but Thou, O Lord God, my Saviour, to whom I commit myself and all that is mine, that Thou mayest keep me and bring me to life everlasting.

[1] Matthew xi, 28.
[2] Genesis iii, 19.

Receive me, for the praise and glory of Thy Name, who hast prepared Thy Body and Blood for my meat and drink.

Grant, O Lord God of my salvation, that by the frequenting of Thy Mystery I may grow in love and devotion.

CHAPTER 5

OF THE DIGNITY OF THIS SACRAMENT, AND OF THE PRIESTLY STATE

THE VOICE OF THE BELOVED

HAD you the purity of an Angel and the sanctity of St. John the Baptist, you would not be worthy to receive or handle this Sacrament.

For it is not due to any human merits that a man should consecrate and handle the Sacrament of Christ and receive for his food the Bread of Angels.

High is the ministry and great the dignity of Priests, to whom is given that which is not granted to the Angels.

For it is Priests alone, duly ordained in the Church, who have the power of celebrating Mass and of consecrating the Body of Christ.

The Priest is in very truth the minister of God: he uses the words of God, and works at the commandment and by the institution of God. And, throughout all his action, the chief author and invisible worker is none other than God, to whose will and commandment everything is subject and everything obedient.

2. Therefore, in this most excellent Sacrament, you ought more to credit God the Omnipotent than any notions of your own or any visible sign. And therefore should you approach this work with fear and reverence.

Take heed to yourself, and see what kind of ministry has been delivered to you by the imposition of the Bishop's hands.[1]

Lo, you have been made a Priest, and consecrated to celebrate Mass. See now that at the due time you offer Sacrifice to God faithfully and devoutly, and that in your life you show yourself free from all blame.

You have not lightened your burden; you are now bound by a stricter bond of discipline, and are obliged to a greater perfection of sanctity.

A Priest ought to be adorned with all virtues, and to set others the example of a good life.

[1] The Roman Pontifical, in the Ordination of Priests.

His conversation should not be with the vulgar and common ways of men, but with the Angels in heaven, or with perfect men upon earth.

3. A Priest, clad in sacred vestments, is Christ's deputy, that he may suppliantly and humbly pray to God both for himself and for the whole people.

He has before and behind the sign of the Lord's cross, that he may ever remember the passion of Christ.

He bears the cross on the front of his chasuble, that he may diligently mark the footsteps of Christ, and fervently endeavour to follow them.

And on the back also he is signed with the cross, that he may for God's sake suffer cheerfully whatever evils be inflicted upon him by others.

He wears the cross in front that he may bewail his own sins; and behind, that he may compassionately lament the sins of others, knowing that he has been made an intermediary between God and the sinner.

Neither ought he to grow weary in prayer and in offering the holy Oblation, until he merit to obtain grace and mercy.

When a Priest celebrates Mass, he honours God, gives joy to the Angels, and edifies the Church. So also he helps the living, obtains rest for the departed, and himself is made partaker of all good things.

CHAPTER 6

HOW SHALL I PREPARE FOR COMMUNION?

THE VOICE OF THE DISCIPLE

When I consider Thy worthiness, O Lord, and my own vileness, I tremble exceedingly and am dismayed.

For if I do not approach Thee, I fly from life; and if I intrude myself unworthily, I incur Thy displeasure.

What then shall I do, O my God, my Helper and my Counsellor in every need?

2. Do Thou teach me the right way; set before me some short exercise suitable for Holy Communion.

For it is well to know how I ought devoutly and reverently to prepare my heart for Thee: for the profitable receiving of Thy Sacrament, as well as for celebrating so great and divine a Sacrifice.

CHAPTER 7

OF EXAMINATION OF CONSCIENCE AND A PURPOSE OF AMENDMENT

THE VOICE OF THE BELOVED

ABOVE all things the Priest of God ought to come to the celebrating, handling, and receiving of this Sacrament with the greatest humility of heart and lowly reverence; with a full faith and a devout intention of doing honour to God.

Examine your conscience diligently, and to the best of your power purge and purify it by true contrition and humble confession; so that you neither have nor know of any grave thing which may give you remorse and hinder your free access.

Be sorry for all your sins in general; and more especially grieve and lament for your daily transgressions.

And if time admit, confess to God, in the secrecy of your heart, all the miseries of your passions.

2. Lament and grieve that you are still so carnal and worldly, and so subject to evil desires;

So full of the motions of concupiscence, so unguarded in your outward senses and so often entangled with many vain imaginations;

So much inclined to outward things, and so negligent in things inward;

So prone to laughter and dissipation, and so averse from tears and compunction;

So ready for relaxation and the pleasures of the flesh, and so sluggish in austerity and fervour;

So curious to hear news and to see fair sights, and so slow to embrace what is humble and abject;

So covetous to possess much, so niggardly in giving, and so tenacious in retaining;

So inconsiderate in talking, and so reluctant to keep silence;

So undisciplined in character, and so rash in conduct;

So eager for food, and so deaf to God's Word;

So ready for rest, and so slow for work;

So wakeful for idle tales, and so drowsy at sacred vigils;

So hasty to finish prayer, and so wandering in attention;

So negligent about your Office, so lukewarm in saying Mass, and so dry at Communion;

So quickly distracted, and so seldom fully recollected;

So suddenly moved to anger, and so reckless in offending others;

So prone to judge, and so severe in censure;

So joyful in prosperity, and so weak in adversity;

So often proposing many good things, and yet performing so little.

3. Having confessed and bewailed these and other defects of yours with sorrow and great discontent at your own weakness, make a firm purpose of constant amendment of life and of advancing in virtue.

Then with an entire resignation, and with your whole will, offer yourself up on the altar of your heart as a perpetual holocaust to the honour of My Name, faithfully committing to Me both soul and body.

Thus shall you be worthy to approach to offer this Sacrifice to God, and to receive for your salvation the Sacrament of My Body.

4. For there is no worthier oblation nor greater satisfaction for the washing away of sins than to offer yourself purely and entirely to God, together with the Oblation of the Body of Christ, in Mass and Communion.

If a man does what he can, and is truly penitent, as often as he shall approach to Me for pardon and grace, *as I live*, says the Lord, *who desire not the death of a sinner, but rather that he be converted and live, I will not remember his sins any more*, but all shall be forgiven him.[1]

CHAPTER 8

OF THE OBLATION OF CHRIST UPON THE CROSS AND OF THE RESIGNATION OF OURSELVES

THE VOICE OF THE BELOVED

EVEN as, with hands outstretched upon the cross and My body naked, I offered Myself up freely to God the Father for your sins, so that nothing remained in Me that was not wholly turned into a sacrifice of divine propitiation: even so ought you willingly to offer yourself to Me daily in the Mass as a pure and holy oblation, with all your powers and affections and with all possible inward devotion.

What do I require of you more than that you endeavour to resign yourself entirely to Me?

Whatsoever you give besides yourself, I regard not; for I seek not your gift, but you.

2. As it would not suffice you, if you had all things except

[1] Ezechiel xxxiii, 11; xviii, 22.

Me, so neither can it please Me, whatever you give, unless you offer yourself.

Offer yourself to Me, and give your whole self for God, and your offering shall be accepted.

Lo, I offered up Myself wholly to the Father for you; I gave My whole Body and Blood for your food, that I might be all yours, and you might be always Mine.

But if you reserve yourself, and do not offer all freely to My will, your offering is not complete, nor will there be an entire union between us.

Therefore a free oblation of yourself into the hands of God ought to precede all your works, if you would obtain freedom and grace.

For the reason why so few become enlightened and inwardly free, is because they know not how to renounce themselves entirely.

My sentence stands sure: *Unless a man renounce all, he cannot be My disciple.*[1]

Therefore, if you desire to be My disciple, offer yourself up to Me with all your affections.

CHAPTER 9

THAT WE OUGHT TO OFFER OURSELVES AND ALL THAT IS OURS TO GOD, AND TO PRAY FOR ALL

THE VOICE OF THE DISCIPLE

THINE, O Lord, are all things that are in heaven and upon earth.

I desire to offer myself up to Thee as a free oblation, and to remain for ever Thine.

Lord, in the simplicity of my heart I offer myself to Thee this day, as Thy servant for evermore, for Thy service, and for a sacrifice of perpetual praise.

Receive me with this sacred Oblation of Thy precious Body, which I offer to Thee this day in the invisible presence of assisting Angels, that it may be for salvation to me and all Thy people.

2. Lord, I offer to Thee, upon Thy altar of propitiation, all my sins and offences, which I have committed in Thy sight and that of Thy holy Angels, from the day that I was first capable of sin until this hour; that Thou mayest burn and consume them all alike with the fire of Thy charity, and mayest blot

[1] Luke xiv, 33.

out all the stains of my sins, and cleanse my conscience from every offence, and restore Thy grace which I have lost by sin, fully pardoning me all and mercifully receiving me to the kiss of peace.

3. What can I do for my sins but humbly confess and lament them, and incessantly implore Thy forgiveness?

I beseech Thee, hear me in Thy mercy when I stand before Thee, O my God.

All my sins are exceedingly displeasing to me; I will never more commit them; I am sorry for them, and will be sorry for them as long as I live; and I am prepared to do penance and make satisfaction to the utmost of my power.

Forgive me, O my God, forgive me my sins, for the sake of Thy holy Name.

Save my soul, which Thou hast redeemed with Thy precious Blood.[1]

Lo, I commit myself to Thy mercy; I resign myself into Thy hands.

Deal with me according to Thy goodness, not according to my wickedness and iniquity.

4. I offer also to Thee all that is good in me, though it be very little and imperfect: that Thou mayest amend and sanctify it; that Thou mayest make it pleasing and acceptable to Thee, and always be perfecting it more and more; and finally that Thou mayest bring me, a lazy and useless wretch, to a blessed and praiseworthy end.

5. I offer to Thee also all the pious desires of devout persons, the necessities of my parents, friends, brothers, sisters, and all that are dear to me, and of all such as for love of Thee have been benefactors to me or others, and who have desired and besought me to offer up prayers and Masses for themselves and all theirs, whether they are still living in the flesh or are already departed out of this world. So may they all experience the assistance of Thy grace, the help of Thy consolation, protection from dangers, and deliverance from punishment; and thus freed from all evils, may they joyfully pay to Thee a noble tribute of thanksgiving.

6. I also offer to Thee my prayers and sacrifices of propitiation, for those in particular who have in any way injured, grieved, or reviled me, or have inflicted upon me any loss or trouble.

And for all those likewise whom I have at any time grieved, troubled, oppressed, or scandalized, by words or deeds, knowingly or unknowingly; that Thou mayest forgive us all alike our sins and offences one against another.

[1] From the *Te Deum.*

Take, O Lord, from our hearts all suspicion, indignation, anger, and contention, and whatever else may wound charity and lessen brotherly love.

Have mercy, O Lord, have mercy on those that crave Thy mercy; give grace to the needy; and make us such that we may be worthy to enjoy Thy grace, and may make good progress in the way to life everlasting. Amen.

CHAPTER 10

THAT HOLY COMMUNION IS NOT LIGHTLY TO BE FORBORNE

THE VOICE OF THE BELOVED

You ought often to have recourse to the Fountain of grace and divine mercy, to the Fountain of goodness and all purity; that you may be healed of your passions and vices, and may deserve to be made stronger and more vigilant against all the temptations and deceits of the devil.

The enemy, knowing the very great fruit and healing power contained in Holy Communion, strives by every means and opportunity, and with his utmost power, to hinder and withdraw devout and faithful souls.

2. For some people, when they set about preparing themselves for Holy Communion, are then subject to Satan's worst assaults.

That wicked spirit himself (as it is written in Job [1]) comes among the sons of God to trouble them with his wonted malice or make them overfearful and perplexed, that so he may lessen their devotion, or by his assault take away their faith. His purpose is to get them, if he can, to give up Communion altogether, or else to approach with little fervour.

But no attention whatever must be paid to his wiles and fancies, be they never so filthy and hideous; and all such imaginations are to be turned back upon his own head.

The wretch must be contemned and scorned; nor is Holy Communion to be omitted on account of his assaults, or for any disturbance of mind that may ensue.

3. Often also a person is hindered by too great a solicitude for devotion, and by some anxiety or other about his confessions.

But follow the counsel of the wise, and lay aside all anxiety and scruple; for these things hinder the grace of God and destroy the mind's devotion.

[1] i, 6; ii, 1.

Do not abandon Holy Communion for every trifling pertur-
bation or trouble; but rather go quickly to confession, and
freely forgive others all their offences.

And if you have offended any one, humbly crave pardon,
and God will readily forgive you.

4. What good do you get by delaying your confession, or
putting off Holy Communion?

Cleanse your soul as soon as possible, spit out the poison
quickly, and then make haste to take the antidote. You shall
find it better to act thus than to delay long.

Supposing to-day you omit Communion for one cause, there
will perhaps be another and a greater one to-morrow; and in
this way you will be a long time without Communion, and
become more and more unfit.

Shake yourself free as quickly as possible from your present
heaviness and sloth. What good do you get by continuing long
in a state of anxiety and disquiet, and because of daily obstacles
keeping away from the Divine Mysteries?

On the contrary, it does you much harm to delay Communion for long, because this usually brings on great sluggishness
of soul.

Sad to say, there are some lukewarm and lax people who
are ready to seize any excuse for putting off their confession
and in consequence contrive to postpone Holy Communion.
They are afraid lest they should be obliged to practise more
watchfulness over themselves.

5. How little love of God and what slender devotion have
they who so lightly put off Holy Communion!

How happy is he and how acceptable to God, who lives so
good a life and keeps his conscience so pure, that he is prepared and well disposed to communicate every day, were it
permitted to him and were he able to do so without attracting
too much notice.

If a man sometimes abstains out of humility or because of
some legitimate hindrance, he is to be commended for his
reverent conduct.

But if it be sloth that has crept upon him, let him bestir himself and do his best. Our Lord will second his desire, taking
full account of his good will; for it is the good will that He
chiefly regards.

6. And, even when he is lawfully hindered, he should none
the less have that good will and devout desire to communicate; for in this way he shall not be without the fruit of the
Sacrament.

Indeed, it is open to a devout soul to receive Christ every
day and every hour by the way of a spiritual Communion.

There is nothing to prevent him doing this, and it will be very much to his soul's health.

For as often as a man devoutly dwells upon the mystery of Christ's Incarnation and Passion and thereby is inflamed with His love, so often does he receive Christ spiritually within him and is refreshed invisibly.[1]

Nevertheless, on certain days and at appointed times, he should with a loving reverence receive the Sacramental Body of His Redeemer. And so doing, he ought to seek the honour and glory of God more than his own consolation.

7. But the man that does not prepare himself for Communion except when some festival draws near or custom compels, such a one shall often be unprepared.

Blessed is the man, who as often as he celebrates or communicates, offers himself up as a holocaust to the Lord.

When you celebrate Mass, be neither too slow nor too quick; but observe the good common practice of those with whom you live.

You ought not to cause others to have trouble or tedium. Keep the common way, as established by our fathers. Study to serve the advantage of others rather than your own personal devotion or inclination.

CHAPTER 11

THAT THE BODY OF CHRIST AND THE HOLY SCRIPTURES ARE MOST NECESSARY FOR A FAITHFUL SOUL

THE VOICE OF THE DISCIPLE

O SWEETEST Lord Jesus, how great is the delight of a devout soul that feasts with Thee in Thy banquet, wherein no other food is set before her but Thyself, her only Beloved, desirable beyond every good that her love can desire.

Sweet, indeed, would it be for me, could I from heartfelt love shed tears of devotion in Thy presence, and with loving Magdalen wash Thy feet with those tears.

But what has become of that devotion? Where is that abundant outpouring of tears?

Surely, in the sight of Thee and Thy holy Angels, my whole heart should be aflame with love, and I should weep for very joy.

For in this Sacrament, though Thou art hidden under ap-

[1] William of St Thierry, *Epistle to the Brethren of Mont Dieu*, §30.

pearances that are not Thine own, yet art Thou truly present to me.

2. My eyes could not endure to behold Thee in Thine own divine brightness; neither could the whole world abide the splendour of the glory of Thy Majesty.

In this, therefore, dost Thou consult my weakness, that Thou hidest Thyself under the sacramental veils.

I truly possess and adore Him whom the Angels adore in heaven; I as yet for a while in faith, but they indeed by sight and without any veil.

I must be content with the light of true faith, and walk therein till the day of everlasting glory shall dawn, and the shadows of figures pass away.[1]

But when that which is perfect comes,[2] the use of Sacraments shall cease; for the Blessed in heavenly glory need not any sacramental healing.

For they rejoice without end in the presence of God, beholding His glory face to face. And transformed from glory unto the glory[3] of His unfathomable Godhead, they taste the Word of God made flesh, as He was from the beginning and abides for ever.

3. When I call to mind these wondrous things, there is no spiritual comfort itself, of whatever sort, but becomes very tedious to me; because so long as I behold not my Lord openly in His glory, I make no account of all that I see and hear in the world.

Thou art my witness, O God, that nothing can comfort me, nor anything created give me rest, but only Thou, my God, whom I desire to contemplate for eternity.

But that is not possible so long as I remain in this mortal life.

And therefore I must set myself to much patience, and submit myself to Thee in every desire.

For thus also did Thy Saints, O Lord, who now rejoice with Thee in the Kingdom of Heaven. Whilst they were yet alive, they awaited in faith and much patience the coming of Thy glory.

What they believed, I believe; what they hoped, I hope for; and whither they are arrived, I trust that I also through Thy grace shall arrive.

In the meantime I will walk in faith, being strengthened by the examples of the Saints.

Moreover, I shall have Holy Scripture for my consolation

---

[1] Canticle of Canticles ii, 17.
[2] 1 Corinthians xiii, 10.
[3] 1 Corinthians xiii, 12; 2 Corinthians iii, 18.

and for a mirror of life. And, above all these things, I shall have Thy most Holy Body for a special remedy and refuge.

4. For in this life I find there are two things especially necessary for me, without which this miserable life would be insupportable.

Whilst detained in the prison of this body, I acknowledge that I need two things, namely, food and light.

Therefore hast Thou given me in my weakness Thy Sacred Body for the nourishment of my soul and body; and Thou hast set Thy Word as a lamp to my feet.[1]

Without these two I could not well live; for the Word of God is the light of my soul, and Thy Sacrament is the Bread of Life.

These also may be called the two tables set on either side in the treasury of Holy Church.

The one is the table of the Sacred Altar, having the holy bread, that is, the precious Body of Christ; the other is that of the Divine Law, containing holy doctrine, teaching men the right faith, and leading securely even within the veil,[2] where is the Holy of Holies.

5. Thanks be to Thee, O Lord Jesus, Light of eternal Light, for the table of sacred doctrine, which Thou hast ministered to us by Thy servants, the prophets and apostles, and by other teachers.

Thanks be to Thee, O Thou Creator and Redeemer of men, who to manifest Thy love to the whole world hast prepared a great supper,[3] wherein Thou hast set before us to be eaten, not the typical lamb, but Thy most Holy Body and Blood, rejoicing all the faithful with this sacred banquet and inebriating them with the chalice of salvation, wherein are all the delights of paradise. And the holy Angels do feast with us, but with a more happy sweetness.

6. O how great and honourable is the office of Priests! to whom it is given to consecrate with sacred words the Lord of Majesty, to bless Him with their lips, to hold Him in their hands, to receive Him with their own mouths, and to administer Him to others.

O how clean ought to be those hands, how pure the mouth, how holy the body, how immaculate the heart of the Priest, into whom the Author of Purity so often enters!

From the mouth of a Priest nothing but what is holy, no

[1] Psalm cxviii, 105.
[2] Hebrews vi, 19.
[3] Luke xiv, 16.

word but what is becoming and profitable ought to proceed, who so often receives the Sacrament of Christ.

7. Simple and chaste should be his eyes that are wont to behold the Body of Christ.

Pure and raised to heaven should be his hands which are wont to handle the Creator of heaven and earth.

To Priests especially it is said in the Law, *Be ye holy; for I, the Lord your God, am holy.*[1]

8. Let Thy grace, O God Almighty, assist us, that we who have undertaken the priestly office may be enabled to serve Thee worthily and devoutly, in all purity, and with a good conscience.

And if we cannot live in so great innocence of life as we ought, yet grant us duly to bewail the sins we have committed, and in the spirit of humility, and the purpose of a good will, to serve Thee more fervently for the future.

CHAPTER 12

WITH HOW GREAT DILIGENCE THE COMMUNICANT SHOULD PREPARE HIMSELF FOR CHRIST

THE VOICE OF THE BELOVED

I AM the Lover of purity and the Giver of all sanctity. I seek a pure heart, and there is the place of My rest.

Make ready for Me a large upper room furnished, and with you I will eat the Pasch along with My disciples.[2]

If you will have Me to come to you and remain with you, purge out the old leaven[3] and make clean the habitation of your heart. Shut out the whole world and all the tumult of vices; sit as a sparrow solitary on the house-top;[4] and think of your transgressions in the bitterness of your soul.

For every lover prepares the best and fairest room for his dearly beloved; for thus is known the affection of him that entertains his beloved.

2. Know, nevertheless, that you cannot make sufficient preparation by the merit of any action of yours, even should you prepare yourself for a whole year together, so as to think of nothing else.

But it is of My mere goodness and grace that you are suffered to come to My table; as if a beggar should be invited to

[1] Leviticus xix, 2; xx, 26; 1 Peter i, 16.
[2] Mark xiv, 15.
[3] 1 Corinthians v, 7.
[4] Psalm ci, 8.

the banquet of a rich man, and he had nothing else to return him for his benefits but to humble himself and give him thanks.

Do, therefore, what in you lies, and do it diligently; not out of custom nor from necessity; but with fear, reverence, and affection receive the Body of your beloved Lord, who vouchsafes to come to you.

It is I that have called you; I have commanded it to be done; I will supply what is wanting to you; come and receive Me.

3. When I bestow the grace of devotion, give thangs to your God, not because you are worthy, but because I have had compassion on you.

If you have no devotion but rather find yourself dry, be instant in prayer, sigh and knock; nor desist until you deserve to receive some crumb or drop of saving grace.

You have need of Me, not I of you. Neither do you come to sanctify Me; but I come to sanctify you and make you better.

You come that you may be sanctified by Me and united to Me; that you may receive new grace, and be incited anew to amendment.

Neglect not this grace, but prepare your heart with all diligence, and so welcome your Beloved into your house.

4. But not only ought you to prepare yourself for devotion before Communion; you should also carefully keep yourself therein after you have received the Sacrament. A devout preparation beforehand is necessary; but it is just as necessary that you should afterwards keep guard over yourself. For to keep such guard, and keep it well, is in its turn the best preparation for the obtaining of greater grace.

For if a man presently pours himself out without restraint upon outward comforts, he is thereby rendered very indisposed for devotion.

Beware of much talk; remain in secret and enjoy your God; for you have Him whom the whole world cannot take from you.

I am He to whom you ought to give your whole self; that so you may no longer live in yourself but in Me, and be free from all solicitude.

CHAPTER 13

THAT A DEVOUT SOUL OUGHT TO DESIRE WITH ITS WHOLE HEART TO BE UNITED WITH CHRIST IN THIS SACRAMENT

THE VOICE OF THE DISCIPLE

WHO will grant me, O Lord, to find Thee alone,[1] to open my whole heart to Thee, and to enjoy Thee even as my soul desires? Would that no one may henceforth despise me, nor anything created move or regard me; but that Thou alone mayest speak to me, and I to Thee, as the beloved is wont to speak to his beloved, and a friend to feast with a friend.[2]

For this I pray, this I desire, that I may be wholly united to Thee, that I may withdraw my heart from all things created, and that, by Holy Communion and by frequent celebration of Mass, I may more and more learn to relish things heavenly and eternal.

My Lord and my God! when shall I be wholly united to Thee, and absorbed in Thee, and become altogether forgetful of myself? Thou in me, and I in Thee! Grant that we may abide thus united in one.

2. Verily Thou art my Beloved, chosen out of thousands,[3] in whom my soul is well pleased to dwell all the days of her life.

Verily Thou art my Peace-maker, in whom is sovereign peace and true rest; and out of whom is labour and sorrow and endless misery.

Verily Thou art a hidden God,[4] and Thy counsel is not with the wicked, but with the humble and the simple is Thy speech.

O how sweet is Thy Spirit, O Lord, who to show Thy sweetness towards Thy children, vouchsafest to refresh them with that most delicious bread which comes down from heaven.[5]

Verily no other nation is there so great, or has its gods so nigh to it, as Thou, our God, art present to all Thy faithful; to whom, for their daily solace, and for raising up

[1] Canticle of Canticles viii, 1.
[2] *Ibid.;* Exodus xxxiii, 11.
[3] Canticle of Canticles v, 10.
[4] Isaias xlv, 15.
[5] St Thomas Aquinas (using Deuteronomy iv, 6) in the Office of Corpus Christi.

their hearts to heaven, Thou givest Thyself to be eaten and enjoyed.[1]

3. For what other nation is there so renowned[2] as the Christian people?

Or what creature under heaven is so beloved as a devout soul, to whom God comes that He may feed it with His own glorious flesh? O unspeakable grace! O wonderful condescension! O boundless love bestowed singularly on man!

But what return shall I make to the Lord[3] for this grace, for such excelling love?

There is nothing that I can do more acceptable than to give up my heart entirely to God, and closely unite it to Him.

All that is within me shall rejoice exceedingly, when my soul is perfectly united to God. Then will He say to me: If thou wilt be with Me, I will be with thee. And I shall answer Him: Vouchsafe, O Lord, to remain with me; I will willingly abide with Thee.

This is my whole desire, that my heart may be united to Thee.

CHAPTER 14

HOW ARDENTLY SOME DEVOUT PERSONS LONG FOR THE BODY OF CHRIST

THE VOICE OF THE DISCIPLE

O HOW *great is the multitude of Thy sweetness, O Lord, which Thou hast hidden for them that fear Thee!*[4]

When I call to mind those devout persons, O Lord, who approach Thy Sacrament with the greatest devotion and affection, then am I often put to shame, and I blush that I approach so tepidly and coldly to Thy Altar, and to the Table of Holy Communion. Alas! that I remain so dry and without affection of heart, that I am not wholly set on fire in Thy presence, O my God, nor so vehemently attracted and affected as many devout persons have been. Such was their exceeding desire of Communion and heartfelt love that they could not restrain their tears, but with the mouth both of heart and body did from the very depths of their soul yearn for Thee, O God, the Fountain of Life, and could not

[1] *Loc. Cit.*
[2] Deuteronomy iv, 8.
[3] Psalm cxv, 3.
[4] Psalm xxx, 20.

allay or satisfy their hunger otherwise than by receiving Thy Body, with all joy and spiritual eagerness.

2. What a truly burning faith is theirs! and what a persuasive evidence of Thy sacred Presence!

Truly do they know their Lord in the breaking of bread, whose heart burns so mightily within them because Jesus is walking with them.[1]

Far from me too often is such affection and devotion, such vehement love and ardour.

Be Thou merciful to me, O good and sweet and gracious Jesus, and at least sometimes grant this poor beggar of Thine, when he comes to Holy Communion, to feel some measure of the heartfelt affection of Thy love.

So may my faith be strengthened, my hope in Thy goodness increased, and may my charity, that has once been perfectly enkindled in the experience of the heavenly Manna, never suffer any failure.

3. For Thy mercy is able to give the grace which I desire, and in Thy great clemency to visit me with the spirit of fervour, when the day of Thy good pleasure comes.

For though I burn not with so great a desire as Thy special devoted clients, yet by Thy grace I do desire that great and burning desire. It is my prayer and my desire that I may have part with all such fervent lovers of Thine, and may be numbered in their holy company.[2]

CHAPTER 15

THAT THE GRACE OF DEVOTION IS ACQUIRED BY HUMILITY AND SELF-DENIAL

THE VOICE OF THE BELOVED

You ought to seek the grace of devotion earnestly, to ask for it fervently, to wait for it patiently and confidently, to receive it thankfully, to keep it humbly, to work with it diligently, and while awaiting its coming, to commit to God the time and manner of the heavenly visitation.

You ought especially to humble yourself when you feel inwardly little or no devotion, and yet not be too much dejected, nor grieve inordinately.

God often gives in one short moment what He has for a long time denied.

[1] Luke xxiv, 30-35.
[2] William of St Thierry, *Meditatio xii.*

At the end of prayer He sometimes gives what at the beginning He put off giving.

2. If grace were always given at once, and were forthcoming when desired, weak man could not well bear it.

Therefore the grace of devotion must be awaited with good hope and humble patience. Yet impute it to yourself and to your sins when it is not given, or when it is secretly taken away.

It is sometimes a trifling matter that hinders and hides grace; if indeed that should be called trifling, and not rather weighty, which prevents so great a good.

And if you will remove this thing, be it little or great, and perfectly overcome it, you shall have your desire.

3. For as soon as you deliver yourself up to God with your whole heart, and neither seek this nor that for your own pleasure or will, but place yourself wholly in His hands, you shall find yourself united and at peace. For nothing will be so grateful to you and please you so much as the good pleasure of the Divine will.

Whosoever, therefore, with simplicity of heart shall lift up his intention to God, and empty himself of all inordinate love or dislike for any created thing, he shall be very fit to receive grace and worthy of the gift of devotion.

For the Lord bestows His blessing there where he finds the vessels empty.

And the more perfectly a man forsakes the things below, and the more he dies to self by contempt of himself, the more speedily does grace come, the more plentifully it enters in, and the higher it elevates the heart that is free.

4. Then shall he see and abound, and shall admire, and his heart shall be enlarged[1] within him, because the hand of the Lord is with him, and he has put himself wholly into His hands for ever.

Behold, thus shall the man be blessed who seeks God with his whole heart, and receives not his soul in vain.[2]

Such a one, in receiving the Holy Eucharist, obtains the great grace of divine union; because he does not regard his own devotion and consolation, but above all devotion and consolation regards the honour and glory of God.

[1] Isaias lx, 5.
[2] Psalm cxxvii, 4; cxviii, 2; xxiii, 4.

CHAPTER 16

THAT WE SHOULD LAY OPEN OUR NECESSITIES TO CHRIST AND CRAVE HIS GRACE

THE VOICE OF THE DISCIPLE

O MOST sweet and most loving Lord, whom I now desire to receive with all devotion! Thou knowest my infirmity and the necessity which I endure; under how great evils and vices I lie prostrate; how often I am oppressed, tempted, troubled, and defiled.

To Thee do I come for remedy, to Thee do I pray for consolation and relief. I speak to Him who knoweth all things, to whom all my inward life is manifest, and who alone can perfectly console and assist me.

Thou knowest what good things I stand most in need of, and how poor I am in virtues.

2. Behold, I stand before Thee poor and naked, begging grace and imploring mercy.

Feed Thy hungry beggar, inflame my coldness with the fire of Thy love, enlighten my blindness with the brightness of Thy Presence.

Turn for me all earthly things into bitterness, all things grievous and cross into patience, and all base and created things into contempt and oblivion.

Lift up my heart to Thee in heaven, and suffer me not to wander upon earth.

Mayest Thou alone be sweet unto me henceforth and for evermore.

For Thou only art my meat and drink, my love and my joy, my sweetness and my whole good.

3. O that with Thy Presence Thou wouldst totally inflame, consume, and transform me into Thyself, that I may be made one spirit with Thee by the grace of inward union, and by the melting of ardent love!

Suffer me not to go from Thee hungry and dry; but deal mercifully with me, as Thou hast often dealt so wonderfully with Thy Saints.

What marvel if I should become wholly on fire with Thee, and in myself should fail and die away? For Thou art Fire ever burning and never failing; Thou art Love purifying the heart and giving light to the mind.

CHAPTER 17

OF A BURNING LOVE AND VEHEMENT DESIRE TO RECEIVE CHRIST

THE VOICE OF THE DISCIPLE

WITH deepest devotion and burning love, with all affection and fervour of heart, I desire to receive Thee, O Lord, even as many Saints and devout persons have desired Thee when they were to receive Communion. They indeed were most pleasing to Thee by the holiness of their lives, and in devotion they were exceeding fervent.

O my God, my Eternal Love, my whole good and never ending happiness! I long to receive Thee with the most vehement desire and most worthy reverence that any of the Saints have ever had or could experience.

2. And although I am unworthy to possess all the devout feelings of the Saints, nevertheless I offer Thee the whole affection of my heart, as if I in my single self had all of those most acceptable ardent desires.

Yes, and all that a devout mind can conceive and desire, all this with the deepest reverence and most inward fervour do I present and offer to Thee.

I desire to hold back nothing for myself, but freely and most willingly to immolate to Thee myself and all that is mine.

O Lord my God, my Creator and Redeemer, I desire to receive Thee this day with such affection, reverence, praise, and honour, with such gratitude, worthiness, and love, with such faith, hope, and purity, as that wherewith Thy most holy Mother, the glorious Virgin Mary, received and desired Thee, when to the Angel who brought her the glad tidings of the Mystery of the Incarnation, she humbly and devoutly answered: *Behold the handmaid of the Lord; be it done unto me according to thy word.*[1]

3. And even as Thy blessed Precursor, the most excellent among the Saints, John the Baptist, rejoicing in Thy presence, leapt through joy of the Holy Ghost whilst he was yet enclosed within his mother's womb; and afterwards, seeing Jesus walking among men, humbling himself exceedingly said with devout affection: *The friend of the bridegroom, who stands and hears Him, rejoices with joy because of the bridegroom's voice:*[2] even

[1] Luke i, 38.
[2] John iii, 29.

so do I wish to be on fire with great and holy desires, and to offer myself to Thee with my whole heart.

Wherefore also I here offer and present to Thee the rejoicings of all devout hearts, their ardent affections, their ecstasies, supernatural illuminations, and heavenly visions, together with all the virtues and praises that have been or shall be celebrated by all creatures in heaven and earth, for myself and all such as have been recommended to my prayers; in order that Thou mayest worthily be praised by all and for ever glorified.

4. Receive my vows, O Lord my God, and my desires of giving Thee infinite praise and boundless blessing, which according to the immensity of Thy unspeakable greatness are most justly due to Thee.

These I render and desire to render to Thee every day and every moment of time; and with my prayers and affections I invite and entreat all the Heavenly Spirits, and all Thy Faithful to join me in rendering to Thee thanksgiving and praise.

5. Let all peoples, tribes, and tongues praise Thee, and magnify Thy holy and most sweet Name, with highest jubilation and with ardent devotion.

And may all, whoever reverently and devoutly celebrate Thy most high Sacrament, and receive It with full faith, deserve to find grace and mercy at Thy hands; and let them pray suppliantly for me a sinner.

And when, having obtained this desired devotion and blissful union, they go from Thy sacred heavenly Table fully comforted and wondrously refreshed, let them vouchsafe to remember me, who am so poor.

CHAPTER 18

THAT A MAN SHOULD NOT BE A CURIOUS SEARCHER INTO THIS SACRAMENT, BUT A HUMBLE FOLLOWER OF CHRIST, SUBMITTING HIS VIEWS TO HOLY FAITH

THE VOICE OF THE BELOVED

You must beware of curious and useless scrutiny into this most profound Sacrament, if you would not be plunged into the depths of doubt.

He that is a searcher of majesty shall be overwhelmed by glory.

God is able to effect more than man can understand.

A devout and humble inquiry after truth is allowable, if it be ever ready to be taught and if it seek to walk according to the sound teachings of the Fathers.

2. Blessed is that simplicity which leaves the difficult paths of questionings, and goes on in the plain and sure path of God's commandments.

Many have lost devotion whilst they would search into lofty matters.

It is faith and an upright life that are required of you; not loftiness of understanding nor the profundities of the mysteries of God.

If you neither understand nor comprehend those things which are beneath you, how shall you comprehend those that are above you?

Submit yourself to God, and humble your opinion to faith. Then the light of knowledge shall be given you, according as shall be profitable and necessary for you.

3. Some are grievously tempted concerning faith and the Sacrament; but that is not to be imputed to them, but rather to the enemy.

Be not anxious, nor stop to dispute with your thoughts, nor answer doubts which the devil suggests; but believe the words of God, believe His Saints and Prophets, and the wicked enemy shall fly from you.

It is often very profitable that the servant of God should suffer such things.

For the devil does not tempt unbelievers and sinners, whom he already securely possesses; but the faithful and devout he tempts and molests in many ways.

4. Go forward, therefore, with a simple and undoubting faith, and with lowly reverence approach the Sacrament; and whatsoever you are not able to understand, securely commit to God Almighty.

God does not deceive you; but that man is deceived who trusts too much to himself.

God walks with the simple, reveals Himself to the humble, and gives understanding to little ones. He discloses His meaning to pure minds, and hides His grace from the curious and proud.

Human reason is weak and may be deceived; but true faith cannot be deceived.

5. All reason and natural investigation ought to follow faith, and not go before or infringe upon it.

For faith and love are here most especially predominant;

and they work by hidden ways in this most holy and supremely excellent Sacrament.

God, who is eternal and incomprehensible and of infinite power, does things great and inscrutable in heaven and in earth; and there is no searching out His wonderful works.

If the works of God were such that they could easily be comprehended by human reason, they would not rightly be called either wonderful or unspeakable.

THE END

INDEX

Adversity, the uses of, 27-28, 32,111; to be borne patiently, 88, 96-97, 116-7; the example of Christ, 95. *See* Cross.

Advice, better to receive than to give, 25; value of good advice, 22, 29, 82, 171-2.

Affections, inordinate, 22, 56, 87, 113,141.

Agatha, St, 126.

Ambition, 58-59, 104.

Amendment of life, 48-51.

Apostles, their example, 33-34, 101.

Avarice, 22-23.

Bethany, 115.

Books, which to be read and how, 22; the Scriptures especially necessary for us, 173-5.

Cares, to be cast on God, 94; freedom from, 106-7.

Cell, to be frequented, 38-39.

Christ, *see* Jesus Christ.

Communion, *see* Holy Communion.

Compunction, 17, 38, 39-41, 139-40.

Concupiscence, 88-9.

Confession, 80, 162, 171.

Conscience, joy of a good, 38, 58-59.

Consolation and Desolation, 62-64, 72-74, 75, 79-80, 82, 89, 93, 139.

Contempt of self, 18-19; of pleasures and honours, 52-53, 113-14, 123. *See* Humility.

Conversation, with God, 52-54, 60-61; with men, 24, 38-39, 55-56, 166.

Courage, 148.

Cross of Jesus, to be loved and carried with patience and joy, 66-71, 147-8.

Curiosity, about the affairs of others, 104; about difficult matters, 125, 150-3, 184-6.

David, King, his devotion, 157.

Death, meditation on, 37, 43-45.

Defects, our own to be considered rather than those of others, 32, 57.

Desolation, 62-64, 99, 106, 136-8.

Detachment from creatures, 112-13, 141.

Devil, 80-81, 89, 171.

Devotion, prayer for, 75; to be concealed, 81-2; towards the Eucharist, 179-80, 183-4.

Enlightening of the mind, prayer for, 103-4.

Eternity, the day of, 131-2; desire of, 133-5.

Eucharist, the Holy, *see* Holy Communion *and* Mass.

Examination of conscience, 36, 167-68.

Example, of Christ, 89-90, 95; of the Saints, 33-4, 151; of good men, 49-50.

External things, how to be used, 120-21, 125-26.

Familiarity, excessive, to be avoided, 24.

Fervour, 48-51.

Francis of Assisi, St, 138.

Friendship with Jesus, to be sought above all, 59-62, 104, 127, 141, 154.

God, our final end, 84-85, 115; without Him we are nothing, 90-91, 112, 121; our peace and comfort, 93, 98-100, 110-11, 115-16, 137; all our trust to be placed in Him, 153-54.

Grace, 64-6; to be guarded by humility, 81-82; not given to worldlings, 140-41; contrasted with nature, 142-46.

Heaven, the glory of, 47-8, 75, 80, 130, 131, 132, 133-35, 151, 174.

Hell, 41, 46-8, 88, 140.

The Mentor Religious Classics

THE HOLY BIBLE IN BRIEF *edited and arranged by James Reeves*

The basic story of the Old and New Testaments told as one clear, continuous narrative. (#MD116—50¢)

THE PAPAL ENCYCLICALS In Their Historical Context *edited by Anne Fremantle*

The teachings of the Catholic Church as expressed by the Popes in their official letters. (#MT256—75¢)

THE MEANING OF THE GLORIOUS KORAN. *An explanatory translation by Mohammed Marmaduke Pickthall*

The complete sacred book of Mohammedanism, translated with reverence and scholarship. (#MT223—75¢)

THE SONG OF GOD: BHAGAVAD-GITA *with an Introduction by Aldous Huxley*

The Hindu epic translated by Swami Prabhavananda and Christopher Isherwood. (#MD103—50¢)

THE SAYINGS OF CONFUCIUS, *a new translation by James R. Ware*

The sayings of the greatest wise man of ancient China. (#MD151—50¢)

THE TEACHINGS OF THE COMPASSIONATE BUDDHA *edited, with commentary, by E. A. Burtt*

The basic texts and scriptures, early discourses. The Dhammapada, and later writings of Buddhism. (#MD131—50¢)

THE LIVING TALMUD: The Wisdom of the Fathers and Its Classical Commentaries, *selected and translated by Judah Goldin*

The religious and ethical teachings of the Old Testament as interpreted by ancient prophets and scholars—newly translated. (#MT286—75¢)

The Mentor Philosophers

The entire range of Western speculative thinking from the Middle Ages to modern times is presented in this series of six volumes. "A very important and interesting series."—*Gilbert Highet*

50 cents each

THE AGE OF BELIEF: The Medieval Philosophers
edited by Anne Fremantle.   (#MD126)
"Highly commendable . . . provides an excellent beginning volume."   —*The Classical Bulletin*

THE AGE OF ADVENTURE: The Renaissance Philosophers
edited by Giorgio de Santillana.   (#MD184)
"The most exciting and varied in the series."
            —*New York Times*

THE AGE OF REASON: The 17th Century Philosophers
edited by Stuart Hampshire.   (#MD158)
"His (Hampshire's) book is a most satisfying addition to an excellent series."   —*Saturday Review*

THE AGE OF ENLIGHTENMENT: The 18th Century Philosophers *edited by Sir Isaiah Berlin.*   (#MD172)
"(Sir Isaiah) has one of the liveliest and most stimulating minds among contemporary philosophers."
            —*N. Y. Herald Tribune*

THE AGE OF IDEOLOGY: The 19th Century Philosophers
edited by Henry D. Aiken.   (#MD185)
". . . perhaps the most distinct intellectual contribution made in the series."   —*New York Times*

THE AGE OF ANALYSIS: 20th Century Philosophers
edited by Morton White.   (#MD142)
"No other book remotely rivals this as the best available introduction to 20th century philosophy."
            —*N. Y. Herald Tribune*

The Classics and Criticism